MESSIAH'S

THRONE AND KINGDOM;

OR, THE

LOCALITY, EXTENT, AND PERPETUITY

OF

CHRIST'S KINGDOM.

BY REV. J. HARKNESS,

PASTOR OF THE FIRST PRESBYTERIAN CHURCH, FISHKILL LANDING.

NEW YORK:
JOHN MOFFET, 82 NASSAU STREET.

1855.

R. CRAIGHEAD, Printer and Stereotyper,
53 Vesey street, New York.

PREFACE.

The Bible is a good book. It is the best book. It is God's book. It contains a glorious system of doctrine involving the salvation of men, the redemption of the world, and the glory of its Author. It gives an epitomized history of the past, and also, by prophecy, of the future. In it, the curtain is lifted by divine hands, and the yet to be, exhibited to view and contemplation. By descriptions, figures, and symbols panorama-like it passes before us the great convulsions which have yet to agitate the nations, the tumults which have to distract and perplex the people: the terrible hosts which have to be gathered together to battle from the war-mad nations of the earth; the oceans of blood which have to be shed; and the enormous multitudes of slain to be strewn on the fields of conflict. It exhibits the onward progress of these things, and represents them as darkening in horror, until the day of the Lord dawns, and the Son of man comes to the redemption of His own long, long suffering people; and this groaning earth, trodden down, oppressed, cursed by Satan its hellish god for six thousand years; and consequently ought to be studied by all.

It is a great mistake to say that prophecy is a dark subject, difficult to be understood, cannot be understood; and therefore it is labour in vain to study it. Such is a reflection upon the wisdom of God, who has given us this large portion of His word; and a daring impeachment of His veracity, who has said, that *all* Scripture, and consequently *the prophetic portion of Scripture*, "is profitable for doctrine, for reproof, for correction, for instruction in righteousness;" 2 Tim. iii. 16. Many prophecies are easy to be understood, while others are more difficult, but the difficulty of some is no reason for abandoning the study of all, or of any; but on the contrary a strong argument for undertaking and prosecuting it with prayerful vigour and perseverance. And this labour shall be crowned with an abundant reward; for it is written, "Blessed is he that readeth, and they that hear the words of this prophecy, and keep these things which are written therein; for the time is at hand," Rev. i. 3. But the man who declines the study of prophecy because it is difficult to be understood, virtually takes it away from the Bible—throws it aside branding it as worthless, though the voice of God may be heard from that which is rejected, uttering the awful doom of the rejecter: "If any man shall take away from the words of the book of this prophecy, God shall take away his part out of the book of life, and out of the holy city, and from the things which are written in this book," Rev. xxii. 19.

Whatever may have been the amount of patient study and prayerful investigation of the prophetic portions of God's word, it would not be saying too much, to say, that it never has received all to which it is entitled. And in too many instances, men who seemingly wished to be candid and unbiassed, have entered upon the study of prophecy with unconscious prepossession in favour of certain views; and consequently, instead of understanding the language in its plain grammatical meaning, they have endeavoured to see in it, and bring out of it, an entirely different meaning—a meaning which the language does not express; and which the fulfilled portions of prophecy do not indicate nor sustain. They have laboured to spiritualize literality out of existence—out of the Bible, and make the future fulfilment of prophecy something very different from the past; and that too, with the interpretations of God's providence withstanding them to the face.

There are perhaps more students of prophecy in the present day than there have been in any other age. The prediction of Daniel is seemingly being fulfilled; "Many shall run to and fro;" that is, many shall endeavour to search out the sense of prophecy, "and knowledge;" that is, the knowledge of prophecy "shall be increased." There are doubtless more prophetic expositions from the pulpit; and never did the press pour forth so many volumes interpreting prophecy, as it is doing at the present day. And it is worthy of notice, that the great majority of these,—almost the whole, many of which are the production of men of great talent, learning, candour and piety—contend for the literal interpretation.

The views presented in the following pages are literal, and the arguments advanced are to establish that interpretation. It is not pretended that there is anything new in these, but simply an exhibition of the truth presented in Scripture. Yet it is confessed that some views are set forth more plainly and extensively than the author has seen them in any work. Many of them were presented to his flock in a course of lectures, and a desire has frequently been expressed to see them in print. After much hesitation he has resolved to lay them before the public. If in the providence of God, they should furnish instruction to any, no matter how few, in the glorious revelations of the Holy Spirit to man; or stir up others to engage in the study of that portion of Holy Writ, he will feel that a great object has been gained. His sole desire is to exhibit the truth of God's word—to set forth the glory yet to be revealed, as foretold by the spirit of prophecy, in all its mighty overwhelming influence, for the conversion of sinners, and the edification of God's people; and his earnest prayer is, that God would bless his humble endeavour.

J. H.

Fishkill Landing, February 24, 1854.

CONTENTS.

CHAPTER I.

David and Messiah's Throne.

CHAPTER II.

Messiah's Kingdom.

CHAPTER III.

THE DURATION OF MESSIAH'S KINGDOM.

CHAPTER IV.

THE TIME WHEN THE KINGDOM SHALL BE GIVEN TO MESSIAH.

CHAPTER V.

BY WHOM THE KINGDOM IS TO BE GIVEN TO MESSIAH.

CHAPTER I.

DAVID AND MESSIAH'S THRONE.

"The Lord God shall give unto him the throne of his father David: and he shall reign over the house of Jacob for ever: and of his kingdom there shall be no end."—LUKE i. 32, 33.

THE angel Gabriel was a distinguished and highly renowned servant of Jehovah. He was repeatedly employed by God to reveal his wonderful purposes of mercy, involving the salvation of a world dead in sin: and "the exceeding and eternal weight of glory" in sure reserve for believers in Christ Jesus. Among these revelations the future and glorious kingdom of Messiah, destined ultimately to destroy and supersede all other great and hoary kingdoms, and endure unrivalled and unshaken for ever, in which redeemed men shall be absolutely holy and supremely blessed; the kingdom of which all the prophets in their turn have spoken, and sung in rapturous strains, and described in glowing language and imagery—to which patriarchs and holy men in every age have, by the eye of faith, looked forward, with longing, burning desire, and fervently wished to see--for the speedy coming of which the faithful upon earth have ever prayed, and are even now, with the same heaven-enkindled desire, praying and sending up one loud and earnest burst of supplication, for which the whole creation now subject to vanity, bondage, the *curse* for man's disobedience, are groaning and travailing in pain together, and are in throes of dreadful agony—for which the souls under the altar, crying for the Lord to avenge their blood, are anxiously waiting—and to which the spirits gathered out of all nations round about the throne are looking forward as their peculiar possession, as their incorruptible inheritance—holds a conspicuous place, and rises up by his divine revelations in matchless beauty and glory to our view. He exhibits that kingdom as the burden, the consummation, the most glorious thing, which by God he was commissioned to reveal. Other truths which he makes known may be like stars in the midnight sky; but this he ushers in and makes it shine like the bright, the morning star; like the rising sun upon a long, dark, dreary night. All the glory of the other truths, like so many streams rolling to the ocean, concentrates here, and shines in united, unclouded blaze. It forms the new, the glorious creation "of the restitution of all things."

Gabriel's eye seems to rest peculiarly upon Messiah's glorious kingdom, and his knowledge of it appears great and extensive, and his views clear and impressive. To him intervening kingdoms have seemingly passed away; a long, unobstructed vista opening far down the future discloses the coming kingdom, and he stands and gazes upon it with thrilling delight, and watches its onward progress. And hence, graphically he describes its coming, the attending magnificent pomp, its unrivalled greatness, its unclouded glory, its unsuffering blessedness, and its endless perpetuity. He, too, represents Jesus the King occupying its lofty and glorious throne; swaying his peaceful sceptre over its far extending domains; subduing all things unto himself; and all in blissful obedience serving him—falling down, joyfully and sincerely worshipping him.

It was the angel Gabriel, so peculiarly instructed in the mysteries of this kingdom, that explained to Daniel his symbolical dream, and those full of trouble visions of his head which he had upon his bed. He informed him, a prince of dreamers, who understood not the visions which passed before his view, nor saw in them a revelation of events, and scenes reaching far into the future, deeply affecting the interests of men and the glory of God, that the four great beasts which he saw were four great kings or kingdoms, which should rise in succession out of the earth, out of this world, out of the wisdom, policy, and prowess of men, and successively destroy each other. He told him, that in the last, or fourth kingdom, which combined in it some of the polity of all the preceding, and which was to be by far the mightiest—"a horn," or emblem of power, "that had eyes and a mouth speaking great things," which is Popery, would arise, and in its antichrist spirit make increasing war with the saints, and prevail against them. That it would manifest towards them burning hatred, and ever thirst for their blood until the Ancient of Days come to destroy this persecuting one, and judgment be given to the persecuted people of the saints of the Most High ; and the time come when the saints, being delivered from his power, and he utterly destroyed, shall possess the kingdom erected by the Lord Jesus Christ upon the ruins of his—upon the earth.

This same angel, so profoundly instructed in Messiah's pre-eminent regal dignity and authority; his kingdom and government yet to be ushered in to the redemption and joy of the whole earth, also explained to Daniel his vision of the ram and the goat. He showed him, that the beasts which appeared in that vision, were symbolical of earthly powers and kingdoms. Thus the last and greatest, the Roman, the antichristian, the papal, combining in it all the evils of popery, and concentrating all its powers of hostility, would engage in conflict with its far superior, the Prince of Peace, and that he would utterly consume and destroy it. That conflict, however, so terrible and destructive in its nature, would not take place till the time of the end. Antichrist would retain possession of his kingdom ; and as the time of its duration drew nearer a close, he would have recourse to cunning, deceptive devices, and crafty stratagems, which would prove successful for extending his dominion, and increasing his power over the hearts and souls of men. He intimated that that power would increase, and with its growing ascendency over the power that kept it in check, would become more bloodthirsty and persecuting, and would, with more unrelenting cruelty, put to death the saints of the Most High. This power, not to be controlled nor changed by the agency of men, would continue till the Son of Man or the Prince of princes came to this earth to consume it by the breath of his mouth—to give it, and them who exercise it, to devouring flame.

Closely connected with all this, and as forming a part of the glorious whole, Gabriel may be viewed as revealing to Daniel the mystery of the resurrection of the body. He showed him the saints sleeping in the earth, reposing in their clay cold beds, waiting the days of their appointed time for their coming change, awaking from its long repose their dust, which had been trodden under the feet of many generations, and nations unnoticed and unknown, becoming instinct with new and immortal life, and hastening together under the strange and wonder-working wisdom and power of God, and forming magnificent structures, fashioned like unto the glorious humanity of Immanuel. Nor do his glorious visions terminate here. The graves of the saints not only appear despoiled of their treasures, and the holy ones who slept therein, alive and enrobed in the righteousness of their Redeemer, but the curtain is lifted, and a scene is disclosed far more magnificent than that which presented itself to the eye of Moses, when he surveyed the Holy Land from the top of Pisgah; or to the eye of Balaam, when he looked upon the goodly tents of Jacob, and the tabernacles of Israel. Messiah's kingdom appears, with the king himself, and his many crowns upon his head, occupying the throne, surrounded by his redeemed ones; his bride supremely happy in the abounding joys of his presence. This magnificent climax—the dawning of a far more glorious dispensation than any that has blessed the earth, since the dark hour that Adam's disobedience blighted and forfeited the joys of Eden—concludes the Book of Daniel, and Gabriel's interpretations and revelations to him.

This great expounder of Daniel's dreams and visions, so far as inspired testimony is concerned, returned to the pavilion of eternity and the presence of his God, and there remained for ages and centuries. For a season at least his labours seemed to be done. No spirit favoured with divine dreams and visions seems to have appeared wrestling before God for an interpreter to expound these; and, consequently, no command was given by Jehovah for Gabriel to fly swiftly to earth as an expounder of such. Centuries rolled on during which Gabriel appears standing before the throne waiting with all eagerness to have his commission renewed, and be sent by God upon errands of prophetic revelation. His eye seems full of earnest watchfulness ; his ear open and listening to catch the very first word of any message that may be intrusted to him ; his ready wing quivers with impatience to fulfil the pleasure of God, in whose presence he stands. The moment at last comes for him to resume his labours ; he is commissioned to earth to the temple at Jerusalem, to Zacharias ministering before the altar of incense, to assure him that his prayer was heard, and that he should have a son, notwithstanding he and his wife were well stricken in years, and instruct him to call his child's name John.

Six months after this God sends him forth again. From the throne of the Eternal he speeds his flight to the obscure city of Nazareth, little known among the cities of the earth ; and to the Virgin Mary of the seed of David, yet less known and renowned among the distinguished and honourable women of the land. To this obscure woman, little if at all known beyond her family circle, though Isaiah had sung of her seven hundred years before, in prophetic rapturous song, Gabriel hastened. He had a message from God, a momentous message, to her and all the world. The few words of that message involved the glorious and momentous burden of all the visions and dreams of Daniel which he explained to him. It announced to Mary the conception, the birth, the name, the future greatness, of the Son of the Highest ; the extent, the glory, and the perpetuity of his kingdom.

The part of the angelic message and prophecy referring to the conception, birth, and name of Messiah, we pass over at present, and proceed to examine and illustrate that portion referring to his regal character and authority. "The Lord God shall give unto him the throne of his father David ; and he shall reign over the house of Jacob for ever ; and of his kingdom there shall be no end."

The angel Gabriel here declares David to be the father of Jesus Christ, of course according to the flesh ; and distinctly teaches that he had been a king, and occupied a throne ; and that this kingdom and throne, once honored by the occupancy and government of David, were yet, by the Lord God, to be given to his Son Jesus, and that Jesus was to sit upon that throne, reign over, rule, and govern that people.

David was the eighth and youngest son of Jesse, and a lineal descendant of Judah, Jacob, Isaac, and Abraham. These his illustrious ancestors, renowned for their strong and unwavering faith, rose up in Goliath-like stature among the believing of their age. Their works, wrought by the mighty power of this divine principle, stand in unrivalled magnitude on earth's historic page. Their deep, vital piety manifested itself in living power in all their conduct, and in their sincere friendship to God. From him in whom they so firmly believed, so fervently loved, and devoutly feared, they received exceeding great and precious promises for themselves and their children. Some of these promises, and the great Abrahamic covenant, have not yet been fulfilled, but doubtless shall be when God's set time comes. The dying Jacob, whose heavenly unscaled eye looked down the long vista of futurity, and through many intervening events, and rested upon the glories of a far remote day, whose blissful hours have not yet appeared on the roll of time, breathed out the following prophetic blessing upon Judah, and through him and his descendants upon the house and family of David, and upon his royal seed too: "Judah, thou art he whom thy brethren shall praise; thy hand shall be on the neck of thine enemies; thy father's children shall bow before *thee*. Judah is a lion's whelp; from the prey, my son, thou art gone up; he stooped down, he crouched as a lion, and as an old lion who shall rouse him? The sceptre shall not depart from Judah, nor the lawgiver from between his feet, until Shiloh come; and unto him shall the gathering of the people be."

In progress of fulfilment of this prophetic benediction, full of glorious meaning, and fraught with the most important and blissful consequences to all subsequent generations—exalting Judah's descendants to regal authority, God commissioned his prophet Samuel to Bethlehem, to anoint one of the sons of Jesse king of Israel. The prophet, in obedience to the divine mandate, having reached the house of that venerablo and pious servant of the Most High, by direct inspiration and divine authority, rejected one son after another, and refused to anoint any as king of Israel till he came to the youngest. David, then a ruddy youth of fifteen years, dreaming and caring little about sceptres, thrones, and kingdoms, was on the plains of Bethlehem keeping his father's flocks, and tending the ewes great with young; tuning his divine, consecrated harp, in sweetest, holiest strains, to the God of Israel, and pouring his pious anthems upon midnight's stilly hour, at the prophet's request was called home. As soon as Samuel saw the beautiful youth standing in his presence, he knew by divine intimation, by the clear revelation of God in his soul, that this was he whom God, in the exercise of his sovereign pleasure, had chosen to be the king of Israel, the successor of Saul; and accordingly, with all the solemnity which the occasion and work required, he "took the horn of oil and anointed him in the midst of his brethren; and the Spirit of the Lord came upon David from that day forward." That act, by the special choice, appointment, and authority of God, made him king of Israel, God's own chosen and anointed king. And while Samuel anointed him with the holy oil, which by divine authority he had prepared, God anointed him with the Holy Ghost, thereby qualifying him for the performance of all the important duties devolving upon him when he should occupy the throne, and rule Israel.

The very manner, then, in which David was chosen and anointed king, strongly prognosticated and insured his future greatness. Chosen of God, and the Spirit of the Lord resting upon him, it was fairly to be presumed that all his plans would be laid in the wisdom and fear of God; that they would be acted out by the omnipotent help of God; and consequently that all his undertakings would be crowned with peculiar success. And that such was the case the whole history of this man, who was a man according to God's own heart, clearly shows and triumphantly proves.

The military valour and skill, and noble conduct of the divinely-anointed David, in all public matters involving the interests of the community, soon gained and secured for him the warm and strong affections of the people. When Saul saw the strong attachment and regard which the people manifested to him whom the Lord had secretly anointed their king, his jealousy was aroused, his hatred was inveterate and vindictive, and, with desperate determination, he resolved upon his murder. Once and again, by various stratagems and feigned madness, he sought to slay him, as if by accident. Failing in one effort, he had recourse to others to put him to death; but God, who had decreed, and by his prophet anointed, him to be the king of Israel, kept him in the hollow of his hand as in a strong fortified tower; guarded him by his invisible and omnipotent providence as by a wall of adamant, so that every plan and attempt of Saul to have him slain signally failed. The plan of "him who rules in the armies of heaven, and among the inhabitants of the earth" was acted out in every respect, and to the fullest extent. All the stratagems of Saul proved abortive in destroying the counsel of God, or subverting his purposes. In due time David was, by the same overruling providence that called him to be, and anointed him king of Israel, and preserved him from Saul's cunning attempts to destroy his life, elevated to rule his people Israel.

After to him many painful and severe trials and dangerous wars, to which it is now unnecessary to advert, David, by the immediate direction of God, who had promised him the kingdom, and by the hand of Samuel anointed him to the office of king, left Ziklag and went up to Hebron, the capital of Judah. When the Lord's chosen appeared in that city, in accordance with the divine purpose, God doubtless working secretly upon their heart, the rulers of that tribe voluntarily chose and anointed him their king. He reigned seven years and six months over the house of Judah ; and during that whole period he might be said to be engaged in contests with the other tribes. At the end of that time they also, without doubt under divine influence upon their hearts, renounced their hostility to him, and chose him to be their king, according to the word of the Lord by Samuel, and sent an embassy to him to that effect. He accepted their proposal, which was in perfect accordance with the purpose of God ; and now, by an overruling providence, carrying out his infinitely wise purposes, he became king of all Israel, and they, the highly honoured and favoured of God, his loyal people. The first act of his reign over the united tribes, was the besieging of Jebus, or Jerusalem, the citadel of which, called Zion, had hitherto remained in the possession of the Jebusites. That stronghold was soon taken by that successful warrior, who never lost a battle; and as the city was conveniently situated in the boundaries of Judah and Benjamin, and in the territory of both, it became the metropolis of the kingdom. Here the royal monarch took up his residence; and upon the sacred hill of Zion, where Abraham's faith was about to offer his son Isaac ages before, built his royal and magnificent palace. Here, in that palace, built upon that holy hill, he erected his throne, or visible kingly seat, "for there were set the thrones of judgment, the thrones of the house of David." It was upon the throne in this palace that he sat dispensing justice and judgment to his people, and ruling over them with his mild and merciful sceptre.

That David had in his palace a throne, or magnificent kingly seat, upon which he appeared in royal attire on certain occasions before the heads, the nobles, and rulers of the people, and for the performance of certain regal duties, admits not of doubt, for such was the custom of the East; and such thrones, or seats, in those days, as well as in the present, had all eastern kings. It were strange, indeed, if David had been an exception from this universal kingly custom, and if while all other kings had their thrones, he had not his! Nor is this made certain merely by eastern habits, but more especially by the sure word of God, which clearly teaches that David had, and did occupy a throne. Again and again, does Scripture make mention of that throne, and abounds with evidence, that while he sat upon that throne he exercised a literal and visible rule over the privileged, the glorious, and far-renowned people of God. The same evidence, also, conclusively proves that this was the *only* throne which David ever occupied. He never had, he never sat upon another. He never sat king upon any other throne, or any other kind of throne than this.

And doubtless this throne, which was the throne of Israel to which David was raised by divine and immediate interposition, as we have seen, was the most noble and honourable of all earthly thrones, and shall be had in delightful and everlasting remembrance, when all others have crumbled into dust, and been buried in hoary oblivion; for it was the throne of Jerusalem, the city of the great king; the throne of the most distinguished and exalted people, the people of Israel, the chosen nation of the Lord, "to whom pertained the adoption, and the covenants, and the promises." Upon that literal throne, the throne of God's chosen people, Israel, David literally sat; and over that people and kingdom he literally reigned three and thirty years, as history, both sacred and profane, clearly testifies.

Now, let this important truth be kept in remembrance, that that throne upon which David sat was a literal, *visible, material throne,* in Jerusalem; that the kingdom over which he reigned was a *literal kingdom* upon earth, the territory of Judea, in Asia Minor, whose boundaries are as distinctly defined as those of any *other earthly kingdom;* and that the Israelites, who were the privileged subjects of his government, were *a literal people.* Of the literality of all these no doubt can be entertained, neither can any arguments be adduced to disprove it. With as much rationality might we doubt the literality of any kingly throne now upon the earth, or of the government existing in the present day in any of the old doomed dynasties of Europe. This throne, then, upon which David sat and ruled God's elect nation, was doubtless, according to the proof already adduced, a *literal throne,* and was, as we have already seen, the only throne upon which he ever sat or possessed. The idea of his occupying a *spiritual throne,* or ruling or reigning *spiritually* in the hearts of the people of Israel, is so preposterous and absurd, and we might add blasphemous withal, if it ever entered into any mind, that it is unworthy of a grave reply. It was, then, of the *literal* throne of Israel in Jerusalem upon which David sat that the angel Gabriel, speaking by the Holy Ghost, said, and the declaration must ever be regarded as the words of soberness, and truth, and inspiration, the words of God himself: "The Lord God shall give unto the Son of the Highest," Jesus Christ, "the *throne* of his father David."

Here, then, we have, from the lips of the divinely-commissioned Gabriel, a solemn promise to the Virgin Mary, that the Lord God would give to the Son to whom she was to give birth the throne of David. Now, as to the fulfilment of the prediction and promise no doubt can be entertained. They must, they will be fulfilled, for the Lord's word shall stand, and he will do all his pleasure. He will not alter nor change the thing that has gone out of his mouth. Though the time of fulfilment should seem to tarry, yet it will come, and come too at the set time, for God cannot forget nor disavow his promise, neither can he break or profane his covenant. The question, then, is not, Will the Lord fulfil his promise; will he give to the Son of the Virgin, Jesus Christ, the throne of his father David? the question is, *How* will he do it? Shall this prediction and covenant be *spiritually* or *literally* fulfilled? Shall Christ sit spiritually and reign spiritually; or shall he sit literally and reign literally upon his father David's throne?

The question just proposed is a very important one, and, in some respects, a difficult one to be satisfactorily answered, because men of learning, piety, and talents are to be found on each side, and advocating with equal zeal the opposing views. Some contend that the prediction will be *spiritually*, some that it will be *literally* fulfilled. This is a subject that has been keenly debated since the days of Origen, the great and perhaps first *allegorist*, and the debate is not yet ended, for interpreters of the Scriptures are yet propounding and endeavouring to prove as scriptural their conflicting views.

Those who contend for the spiritual interpretation of the passage, deny, that Jesus Christ will ever sit personally, that is, as God-man, in glorified humanity upon the rebuilt throne of his father David, and reign visibly in Jerusalem over the house of Jacob, or Heaven's highly-favoured people, Israel; or that he will ever appear in person a reigning king upon the earth; and maintain that he will only sit spiritually, and reign spiritually, upon David's throne, and have in them and over them a spiritual kingdom; they maintain that Christ will not be upon earth, will not have any visible throne upon earth, will not be a visible reigning king upon earth, but that he will reign only by his Spirit in the hearts of his people. Now that Jesus Christ will reign spiritually over his people by his Holy Spirit working by his mighty influences in their hearts is incontrovertibly a truth, and a very important and glorious truth too; but it may be, yes it has been questioned, whether it is *the truth* taught in the prediction; and that is the consideration which now demands attention.

Now, to persuade the unprejudiced mind that this is *the* meaning of the passage, in all fairness it must be shown, that David had a spiritual throne; that he could and did sit spiritually upon that throne; that his government was in verity a spiritual government, and his kingdom a spiritual kingdom; for until this is done it is impossible to see how the prediction can be actually and in verity fulfilled. If David had such a throne, a spiritual throne, surely we need to have it explained what that throne was, and how David, who was a mere man like ourselves, could sit upon that spiritual throne; how material man could occupy a spiritual seat. If David had not such a throne, then this throne, which was not David's, could not be promised to Christ. But David's throne was promised to Christ; and David's throne was, as we have seen, a material throne, consequently it was David's material throne that was promised to Christ; and when this promise is fulfilled Christ must, Christ will, sit upon David's material throne. He cannot sit upon any other, for David never had another; and if he sits upon any other he sits upon what was not David's, and upon what was not implied in the promise, and consequently the promise of God to his Son remains unfulfilled, ever unfulfilled. And when we think of a spiritual throne we think of something we cannot understand; and the more we endeavour to comprehend the idea the more does it elude our comprehension; and it is precisely so with regard to Christ's sitting spiritually upon that throne.

We cannot give up the throne, and the sitting upon that throne, as a mere figure of speech, to accommodate another interpretation, because David had his literal throne, and did literally sit upon that throne, and that throne was the throne promised to the Virgin's Son, and promised certainly that, like his father David, he might sit upon it. This is the plain, grammatical meaning of the passage, and the only idea that would be conveyed to the mind of an unbiased reader. But while we contend for the literality of the throne, and sitting upon the throne, it is not for a moment to be supposed that it is denied, or even insinuated, that Christ does not reign by his Spirit in the hearts and over his people. That is a precious truth, a divine prerogative of Christ, most cordially admitted, and in which we supremely delight, and regard as indispensably necessary to his glory and our being made perfect in holiness. In this way he reigned in the first renewed heart, the heart of Abel, who offered a more acceptable sacrifice than his brother, and for the admission of whose spirit the gates of paradise were first thrown open. And he has so reigned in the heart of every believer, under every dispensation, from that early period to the present hour; and if this is all that is meant by the throne of his father David being given to Jesus, it was only promising to give to him what he already, and had always, possessed. According to this interpretation, nothing new was promised, and nothing new would be given. The promise is indeed without meaning. Nor is the difficulty removed by contending that the reign in this spiritual sense shall be more extensive, shall be over mankind generally, shall be over earth's inhabitants, for the nature of the reign is the same—spiritual, and by the Spirit in the hearts of men. A mere extension of the government, no matter how great that extension may be, cannot in the nature of things change the nature and manner of the government itself, cannot introduce the king himself, and set him personally upon a visible material throne. And surely no man, upon mature reflection, could suppose the Spirit of God capable of such trifling as this; and consequently there seems no clear and Scriptural evidence that the prediction is to be understood spiritually; and that it shall be in verity, and to the fullest extent, fulfilled, by Christ reigning merely in the hearts of his people, or spiritually over them, and without appearing visibly and personally in the midst of them.

But if, after all, it should be asserted and maintained, as perhaps it may be, that Christ is now spiritually occupying David's spiritual throne, and spiritually reigning over the spiritual house of Jacob; and that this reign is destined to increase till it is exercised everywhere, and over every inhabitant of the earth, then we confess our ignorance, and declare that we do not know what the spiritual throne of David means, and humbly ask information. If it should be replied, by way of instruction, "David's spiritual throne is the throne of the believer's heart," we would then ask the wise teacher, Where is this instruction to be obtained?

Is it to be found in the Bible? If so, designate the place, that all may read, learn, and understand. So far as we understand the Bible, the throne of the believer's heart is not the throne of David, but the throne of the Majesty on high—God's throne. If then the throne of the believer's heart be the throne of God, and surely this is what God claims for himself, it must be blasphemy to call God's throne, the throne of David. If this then be a fair and legitimate conclusion, if it be a great Bible truth, then every one who thus spiritualizes the passage is a blasphemer, for he sets David upon the throne of God. But this is a sin from which many who hold the spiritual interpretation, would shrink if they could see it precisely in this light. Nor is this all; but if it be a fair and right interpretation thus to spiritualize the first part of the prophecy, so must it, by parity of reasoning and all sound principles of philology, to interpret every other part of the prophecy. No man who is not under some peculiar bias will deny this. If then spiritualists will have the first part of the prophecy thus interpreted, surely they cannot object, and they have no right to complain, if we interpret what remains according to the same rule. If Christ's sitting upon David's throne, and ruling his people Israel, be spiritual and invisible, then his being born of the Virgin is also spiritual and invisible. And what such a birth would be we pretend not to know, neither of it are we able to form any conception, and therefore leave those who teach and advocate such a mode of expounding the Scriptures to explain. If one act be spiritual, according to the laws of sound philology so must every other in the same passage—his birth as well as his government, his birthplace as well as his kingdom. But if this mode of interpretation is introduced—of spiritualizing when the language is not metaphorical—where shall it end? Where but in the mazes of endless error?

Isaiah speaks of Christ's throne and kingdom, in such language as seems to exclude the very possibility of the idea of their being spiritual or metaphorical, when he says: "For unto us a child is born, unto us a Son is given; and the government shall be upon his shoulder; and his name shall be called Wonderful, Counsellor, the Mighty God, the Everlasting Father, the Prince of Peace. Of the increase of his government and peace there shall be no end, upon the throne of David, and upon his kingdom, to order it, and to establish it with judgment and with justice, from henceforth even for ever." If this language has any meaning it certainly is, that the child born and the Son given shall sit as David did, personally and visibly upon his throne, the throne of Israel; and that he shall reign king of Israel as David did. His government will be like David's, literal, but of a far superior character, being absolutely righteous and holy. It will not do merely to deny that this is the meaning of the passage, and assert that the language is metaphorical and the acts spiritual. It must be proved that the language is metaphorical, and consequently that the throne and government are spiritual. But this involves serious difficulties, inasmuch as all that is here said of his government and the duties which he as king is to perform are evidently—except the phrase "the government shall be upon his shoulder," which intimates that the whole rule is to be on him and by him—to be exercised by him, and not by any other.

But if they will have Christ's throne, kingdom, and government to be spiritual and not literal; then it is but right that they should show divine authority for holding and contending for such a view. Assertion is not sufficient to secure belief. Proof is wanted and demanded. The interpretation is called in question unless they can show, that they have this by special revelation from God, or that all the other parts of the passage are to be metaphorically understood; or that this is in accordance with the interpretation of all prophecy, and its fulfilment too, as far as it has been fulfilled in the course of divine providence. Taking their rule of interpretation, which would be perfectly fair, and applying it to the other parts of the prophecy, what meaning would be brought out? It would teach that Jesus Christ was Spiritually born. But in what sense can the Son of the Virgin, the God-man, be spiritually born? He was flesh of our flesh, really and truly man, and how could his birth, when born of Mary, be a spiritual or metaphorical birth? How could this the Son, really man as well as God, be given spiritually to the Israelites as a Son? Imagination and intellect must equally fail in explaining these difficulties, which have their origin in the spiritualizing system of exposition. But perhaps it may be replied, these are to be understood literally. If so, then all acknowledged rules of interpretation are thrown aside, or set at defiance, and *caprice* is made the standard. And still further, if we are to understand His name, "Wonderful, Counsellor; the mighty God, the Everlasting Father, the Prince of Peace," as here given spiritually, what is the conclusion to which we will be led? Simply this—that if they are to be understood spiritually they are not literally true. This is beyond all controversy the case. Then, if the various appellations here given as the name of Christ are not literally true, he is not, he cannot be a divine person. He is not God, but only in some respects, it may be difficult to say what, like him. This is an awful and revolting conclusion, and yet it is the conclusion to which we are inevitably led by the spiritualizing mode of interpretation.

Nor is this all; but this spiritualizing system of interpretation flatly contradicts the plain statement of the Spirit of God in the prediction. It denies that a child has been, or can be born; that a Son has been, or can be given; that, of the increase of his government and peace, there shall be no end; that there has been, or ever can be, one to whom all these divine titles can be justly and righteously applied; and that there ever shall be such a Kingdom as He is said to establish and govern. This is no vague, rash assertion, no illegitimate conclusion, but on the contrary the only conclusion to which the spiritualizing interpretation conducts. And if this be so, is the spiritual interpretation to be regarded as sound, and to be implicitly received? Are we to believe after all this that Christ is to have no literal, no personal reign on earth; but that He is only to reign in the hearts of His people?

But it is also taught in Scripture, that the saints are to sit with Christ upon his throne, and reign with Him in His Kingdom. This is the privilege of all them, who overcome, or are victorious over their foes. Now if the spiritual interpretation be correct, namely, that by sitting upon the throne of His father David, is meant, that He shall sit upon the throne of the heart of His people, then all the victorious multitude who, by his blood and abounding grace, have overcome their enemies, shall sit with Him upon that same throne; that is to say, multitudes of saints shall sit upon the throne of the heart of saints, upon the throne of their own hearts! and these same multitudes shall reign with Him in the hearts of His believing people. Strange doctrine! Saints sitting upon the throne of the heart of saints, upon the throne of their own hearts! Saints reigning in the heart of saints! It is difficult to understand and believe this. Nay, its palpable absurdity is sufficient to secure its rejection. If we admit the literal interpretation the difficulties in a great measure vanish. We can in some measure see and understand how the saints can be co-enthroned, and co-regnant with Christ—how they are to participate in the government of His Kingdom.

The language of Gabriel to Mary is not metaphorical, but *literal;* and if something more were not meant than the spiritual reign which Jesus Christ has ever exercised by His Spirit in the hearts of His people, why make mention of the throne of David? The very mention of that throne leads us back to something literal and intimates, that when what is here spoken of is fulfilled, it will be literally fulfilled. And for what other reason did Peter make mention of God "having sworn with an oath to David, that of the fruit of his loins, according to the flesh, he would raise up Christ to sit upon His throne?" If a purely spiritual reign were meant, that could have been declared, and set forth in all its importance to the world, without any reference to the throne of David. But the fruit of David's loins according to the flesh, that is the human nature of Christ, God bound himself by an oath to raise up to sit on David's throne. Now, if by David's throne is to be understood the human heart, it may well be asked, how is God to fulfil this engagement made by solemn oath? How is the raised up humanity of Jesus Christ to sit in the hearts of men? If it is replied spiritually, the difficulty is not removed; the question still occurs, how will the humanity of Jesus, for it was his humanity that was raised up for that purpose, sit spiritually in the hearts of his people? If it be the throne of the heart that is meant by David's throne, then beyond all controversy the humanity of Jesus must sit upon the throne of the heart, else God's oath must be worthless, and his raising the humanity of Jesus a vain act. But, for the humanity of Jesus to sit upon the throne of the heart, or in the hearts of His people, seems a physical impossibility, and the attempt to spiritualize this sitting or make it metaphorical seems absurd. And while this spiritual sitting and spiritual reigning, so eagerly contended for, are encumbered with so many and great difficulties, let it be remarked, neither is it clearly taught, nor even obscurely hinted at by Gabriel in the passage, nor is it plainly and indubitably taught anywhere in Scripture, but seems altogether a gratuitous assumption of man—a forced meaning which the passage does not bear ; for it is not shown, either by reason or Scripture, but asserted, that Christ's Kingdom is a spiritual Kingdom, and that He shall reign spiritually over the house of Jacob.

Such an interpretation as a spiritual, or figurative, or metaphorical, to say the least of it, is very questionable ; and what is more, it is neither clearly taught in Scripture, nor evidently implied ; nor does it appear to be in accordance with the analogy of prophecy. It seems to be sustained principally, if not entirely, by the dogmatizing of men, who assume the authority of saying this portion of God's word is to be understood literally, and this portion spiritually, as if the whole matter were to be decided by their judgment and authority, or rather, by their previous tuition, and consequent prejudices or caprice. If, the plain grammatical language of Scripture declare some of God's future purposes, surely it is not for any man to say that what the words express is not their meaning, but that they mean something they do not express, something *not literal*, but *spiritual*, when, if such had been the meaning of the Spirit of God, he could easily have stated it. Others again determined, that the language of Scripture shall speak, and give utterance to their sentiments, put it to the rack and torture of criticism, and by subjecting it to this ordeal, endeavour to convert it into a witness for themselves, and make it give loud and strong expressions, as they suppose, of their views; and accordingly, the literal meaning, in violation of all laws of criticism, is rejected by them. While others, with fewer prejudices, and perhaps more candour and less presumption, are disposed to hear what the Lord God will speak, and learn with the docility of little children the meaning of God's holy word. They take language in its literal acceptation; believe what the words *express*, to be what the Spirit of God means; contend for the *literal* fulfilment of prophecy—the *literal* fulfilment of Gabriel's prophecy, namely, "that the Lord God shall give unto the Son of the Highest the throne of his father David."

We have seen that the spiritual interpretation of this passage is very doubtful; that clear and decided evidence to sustain it is wanting; and what is more, that the obvious meaning of the language employed, and the analogy of prophecy, are against it. It now devolves upon us to inquire if the *literal* interpretation is better sustained. And in order to do this, in a matter of such vast importance, the clear understanding of God's future plans as regards the destiny of the earth, the exaltation of the Jewish nation, and the kingly rule of Messiah over the whole earth, we must reject the dogmatizing teaching, the torturing criticisms, the ingenious explanations of men, who, like Whitby, have a new *hypothesis* which they are determined to support by every aid which they can summon to their assistance; and have respect only to the plain grammatical meaning of language, the clear teachings of the word of God, and the manner in which prophecy has been hitherto fulfilled. With these heavenly lights of the Spirit's own kindling for our guide, and a mind dispossessed of all prejudice, we may, by the assistance of the Holy Spirit, who is able to open the eyes of our understanding, arrive at the true meaning of the passage under consideration, and those of a kindred spirit.

The angel Gabriel, in his enrapturing salutation to Mary, declared, that she, though a virgin, should conceive and bring forth a son, and call his name Jesus. What is here predicted is so completely at variance with all the common and established laws of nature; so directly in opposition to them all, involving a physical and natural impossibility, that surely, if we would have demurred to the literal fulfilment of any prediction, it would have been to the literal fulfilment of this: and we might have asked in unanswerable unbelief, supported by the uniform laws of nature since the creation of man—Will this prediction be *literally* fulfilled? and the very difficulties of the case—the violation of all the laws of nature, would call for ingenuity to explain the difficulty, and furnish some ground for a figurative interpretation. But all such difficulties are removed: all such interpretation is for ever set aside; for the prediction has been fulfilled, and strange as it may seem, it has been *literally* fulfilled. Isaiah sang by inspiration seven hundred and forty years before the event, "Behold a Virgin shall conceive and bear a Son, and shall call his name Immanuel." This prediction was *literally* fulfilled at the birth of Christ, in the stable in Bethlehem; for when that took place, an angel appeared to the shepherds announcing the fulfilment of that prophecy, in these words: "Unto you is born this day, in the city of David, a Saviour, who is Christ the Lord." In this they announced a *literal* birth—the literal birth of a literal manchild; for the Holy thing born of the Virgin was as really and truly a material child as any of woman born. Gabriel foretold also, that his name should be called Jesus; and when circumcised the eighth day according to the law of Moses, that was the name given to him. Here then, we have the clear and indubitable evidence, that a part of Gabriel's prediction—and so far as we can judge, the most difficult part—has been *literally* fulfilled. Nor is this denied, but admitted, by those who contend for the Spiritual interpretation of the other parts of the prophecy. Now we contend, as we think, upon all fair rules of interpretation, that unless we have distinct intimation from the angel, that the subsequent part shall not be literally fulfilled, but fulfilled in a different manner—which intimation we have not, nor anything approaching thereto—then we are shut up to the conclusion, that the remaining, like the preceding, shall be literally fulfilled; that the throne of his father David—the throne which David occupied in Jerusalem, shall be literally given to the Son of the Highest—given to Jesus Christ, and that his humanity descended from David shall sit upon that literal throne.

And still further, in confirmation of this interpretation, let it be remarked, that all the predictions which have been hitherto fulfilled concerning Jesus Christ, to say nothing of other predictions, have been literally fulfilled. And by way of corroborating and illustrating this very important truth, clearly exhibited to view in the providence of God, we may adduce a few instances. Was it predicted by prophets and the angel Gabriel, that Jesus should be born of a Virgin? The prediction according to divine testimony was *literally* fulfilled; wonderful as that literal fulfilment may be, and at variance as it is, with all the laws of nature, and all the births which have hitherto taken place upon the earth. Did Micah sing prophetically, giving utterance to the words of the Holy Ghost, "But thou, Bethlehem Ephratah, though thou be little among the thousands of Judah, yet out of thee shall he come forth unto me, that is to be ruler in Israel; whose goings forth have been of old, from everlasting!" So far as this prophecy has been fulfilled, it will not be denied that it has been literally fulfilled; for Jesus was born in Bethlehem, the very place designated by the prophet, and we cannot entertain a reasonable doubt, that the remaining part shall in like manner be literally fulfilled, when the time for its fulfilment arrives—that Jesus shall as literally rule in Israel; and be a literal King sitting upon David's literal throne, ruling that people gathered from the east and from the west, from the north and from the south, and brought into their own land, as, that, he came out of Bethlehem. Was it predicted in the prophets and in the psalms, that he should be a man of sorrows and acquainted with grief, a prophetic utterance, surely, far more difficult to be believed, than that he should sit in person a King upon David's rebuilt throne? This was literally and awfully fulfilled; for sufferings of every kind and intensity that could possibly afflict sinless humanity, were his portion from the manger to the cross, as every person knows, who has carefully perused his brief history, as recorded by the Evangelists. Was it predicted that he should "ride in triumph into Jerusalem upon an ass, and upon a colt, the foal of an ass?" It was literally fulfilled; for he sent his disciples to bring the colt whereon never man rode, and upon that he entered Jerusalem amidst the Hosannahs of the multitude. Was it predicted that his price should be thirty pieces of silver? The prediction was literally fulfilled; for the chief priests, who were thirsting for his innocent blood and determined upon his death, paid Judas the traitor, thirty pieces of silver to betray him into their hands. Was it prophetically said by the Son of God, many hundred years before his incarnation, "I hid not my face from shame and spitting?" It was literally fulfilled, for the evangelists tell us, they spat upon him in the judgment hall. Was it predicted that the ploughers should plough upon his back, and make long their furrows with the knotty scourge? It was literally fulfilled; for the Roman soldiers scourged him until his back was lacerated in the most dreadful manner. Was it predicted, "He was oppressed and afflicted, yet he opened not his mouth?" It was literally fulfilled, for when he was accused of the chief priests and elders, "he answered nothing." Was it predicted that he should die, and in his death be numbered with transgressors? It was literally fulfilled, for he was crucified between two thieves. Was it predicted that he should be with the rich in his death? It was literally fulfilled; for having no grave of his own, he was buried in the tomb of Joseph, a rich man of Arimathea. Was it predicted that he should not be "left in the grave, neither see corruption?" It was literally fulfilled; for he rose again "the third day according to the Scriptures, and did not see corruption." All these predictions and multitudes more concerning Christ, to which we cannot specifically advert at present, have had their *literal* fulfilment. And surely the literal fulfilment of many of these, seemingly, involves far more and greater difficulties, than Christ's sitting and reigning upon his father David's throne.

And is it predicted, that his father David's throne shall be given to him, and that he shall yet sit upon that throne raised in beauty and magnificence out of its present ruins? It is, and in language clear and distinct—clear and distinct as that of the prophecies which we have just seen have all been literally fulfilled: and how then is this prediction to be understood and fulfilled? From the uniform literal fulfilment of prophecy, we are shut up to the conclusion, that this, too, whatever may be the *seeming* difficulties which stand in the way, unless there is a departure from the uniform procedure of God in the fulfilment of this prediction, will be *literally* fulfilled: and that Jesus Christ, the literal seed of David, the God-man, shall yet sit upon David's literal throne. This literal fulfilment, as we have already seen, is clearly set forth, and strongly argued by Peter under the inspiration of the Holy Spirit, when he contends before the men of Israel, that the crucified humanity of Jesus Christ was raised up from the dead for this very purpose. For says he to the men of Israel, the very men who crucified Him—"David your king, being a prophet and knowing that God had sworn with an oath to him, that of the *fruit of his loins*, according to the flesh, he would raise up Christ *to sit upon his throne:* he seeing this before spake of the resurrection of Christ—of the resurrection of the fruit of his loins. As then, David had a literal throne, a throne upon which he sat while reigning over Israel; and as Christ of the seed of David, who died upon the cross, was literally raised up from the dead—the very body that hung and died upon the cross came up out of the tomb to sit upon *that throne;* according to the very first law of philology, and all consistent interpretation Christ must literally and in person sit upon that throne.

Nor, can it be urged as an unanswerable objection, that the throne of David, so highly honoured by God and so distinctly spoken of here, has been utterly overthrown by the fearful visitations of divine vengeance, which have swept in desolating fury over that land, and Jehovah's privileged people who once dwelt therein—that for many centuries it has been lying in ruins, and trodden down by the feet of barbarous tribes, who in their homeless wanderings have traversed that consecrated soil—that the national existence of the people over whom he ruled has long ago ceased, and that they are now a people scattered among all the nations of the earth, with the brand of Heaven upon their brow, and Jehovah's wrath-cloud over their heads, and Messiah's blood upon their souls, for the guilty rejection and crucifixion of the Son of God. Or to use the truly descriptive language of Scripture (Hos. iii. 4),

"That the children of Israel have abode many days without a king, and without a prince, and without a sacrifice, and without an image, or statue, and without an ephod, and without teraphim;" for all this, instead of being an unanswerable objection, or conclusive proof that Jesus shall not sit upon the throne of his father David, is the standing and divinely perpetuated miraculous evidence, that this very prediction, unfavourable as circumstances, to human view and in human judgment, may seem, shall be literally fulfilled. These desolations of long duration, which seem to militate with such mighty power against the literal exaltation of Jesus to the literal throne, and more than regal kingdom of his father David, shall not endure for aye. When the times of the Gentiles have been fulfilled, and God, in mercy to them, has gathered from among them a people to himself; when they in their turn shall be cut off for their unbelief; and God, in mercy and according to his ancient covenant with Abraham, Isaac, and Jacob, graffs in the Jews again—What then? Hear the language of prophecy—listen to the voice and solemn declaration of God himself: "After that I will return and build again the tabernacle of David, which is fallen down, and I will build again the ruins thereof, and I will set it up." Here God declares he will return to the long forsaken land of Judea, to the dismal desolations of Jerusalem, and the tabernacle of David, and that he will rebuild that tabernacle, that throne, and who will question the adequacy of the omnipotent power of God for the work, or his veracity as regards the declaration. He is doubtless able to do it, and he has said he will do it, and beyond all controversy at the appointed time it will be done. Or to quote the language of Amos, chap. IX. 11, 14, 15, " In that day, will I raise up the tabernacle of David that is fallen down, and close up the breaches thereof: and I will raise up its ruins, and I will build it as in the days of old. And I will bring again the captivity of my people of Israel, and they shall build the waste cities, and inhabit them ; and they shall plant vineyards and drink the wine thereof; they shall also make gardens and eat fruit of them. And I will plant them upon their own land," that is the land promised in covenant to Abraham, and theirs by gift of God. " And they shall no more be pulled up out of their land which I have given them, saith the Lord thy God."

The prophecy preceding this just quoted concerning the utter destruction of the sinful kingdom, but not of the house of Jacob, the sifting of the house of Israel among all nations, their dispersing into every country under heaven, and to the furthest verge of earth, has been literally and awfully fulfilled; as the state of trembling Israel, dispersed and oppressed in every land in the present day, clearly shows. And shall not the prophecy, standing as it does closely connected with this, predicting the gathering of that miserably long scattered people: their restoration to their own land, the land of Canaan, and the enjoyment of every privilege under the kingly government of the Prince of peace, be also literally fulfilled? Shall we not take the exposition, as presented in the providence of God, of the prophecy respecting their dispersion, as the key of exposition of the prophecy of their gathering and restoration? While there is every strong and good reason why we should, surely, there is difficulty in finding any reason why we should not. With this key, then, of interpretation in our hand, we would ask, shall not Jesus literally sit upon the throne of David, raised up from its present ruins by God Almighty himself? For what purpose is the fallen down throne of David to be raised up and erected in more than pristine beauty, grandeur, and immoveable stability? For what purpose are the long dispersed tribes of Israel to be gathered and brought into their own land—the land given to Abraham, Isaac, Jacob, and their seed for ever? but that the promises of God to them, and to the Son of the Highest, may be fulfilled—but that the rebuilt throne of David, and the restored kingdom of Israel, according to the covenant of God with David, may be given unto Jesus the Son of the Highest.

This view, namely the literal, seems supported by Dr. Campbell, the learned and celebrated translator of the Gospels; though he did not believe that Christ would literally sit upon the throne of his father David. In his fifth Dissertation, part 1, §§ 1, 2, 3, upon the phrases, "kingdom of God, and kingdom of heaven," he clearly admits, from the language of the prophets, that Messiah shall have a kingdom; that its locality shall be this earth ; that the God of heaven shall set it up : that having removed all the afflictions of his people, *he shall reign over them in mount Zion.* We give the following quotation ; "In the phrase ἡ βασιλεια τȣ θεȣ, or των ȣρανων, there is a manifest allusion to the predictions in which this economy was revealed by the prophets in the Old Testament, particularly by the prophet Daniel, who mentions it in one place, as a kingdom, βασιλεια, which the God of heaven would set up, and which should never be destroyed ; in another, ch. vii. 13, 14, as a kingdom to be given, with glory and dominion over all people, nations, and languages, to one like a son of man. And the prophet Micah, ch. iv. 6, 7, speaking of the same era, represents it as a time when Jehovah, having removed all the afflictions of his people, would reign over them in Mount Zion, thenceforth even for ever. To the same purpose, though not so explicit, are the declarations of other prophets. To these predictions there is a manifest reference in the title, ἡ βασιλεια τȣ θεȣ, the kingdom of God, or simply ἡ βασιλεια, the kingdom given in the New Testament, to the religious constitution which would obtain under the Messiah. It occurs very often, and is, if I mistake not, uniformly, in the common translation, rendered *kingdom.*"

"§ 2. That the import of the term is always either *kingdom*, or something nearly related to kingdom, is beyond all question ; but it is no less so that, if regard be had to the propriety of our own idiom, and consequently to the perspicuity of our own version, the English word will not answer on every occasion. In most cases βασιλεια answers to the Latin *regnum*. But this word is of more extensive meaning than the English, being equally adapted to express both our terms *reign* and *kingdom*. The first relates to the time or duration of the sovereignty; the second, to the place or country over which it extends. Now, though it is manifest in the gospels that it is much oftener the time than the place that is alluded to, it is never in the common version translated *reign*, but always *kingdom*. Yet the expression is often thereby rendered exceedingly awkward, not to say absurd. Use indeed softens every thing. Hence it is that, in reading our Bible, we are insensible of those improprieties which, in any other book, would strike us at first hearing. Such are those expressions which apply motion to a kingdom, as when mention is made of its *coming*, *approaching*, and the like; but I should not think it worth while to contend for the observance of a scrupulous propriety, if the violation of it did not affect the sense, and lead the reader into mistakes. Now this is, in several instances, the certain consequence of improperly rendering βασιλεια, *kingdom*."

"§ 3. When βασιλεια means *reign*, and is followed by των ουρανων, the translation, *kingdom of heaven*, evidently tends to mislead the reader. Heaven, thus construed with kingdom, ought, in our language, by the rules of grammatical propriety, to denote the region under the kingly government spoken of. But finding, as we advance, that this called the *kingdom of heaven* is actually upon the earth, or, as it were, travelling to the earth, and almost arrived, there necessarily arises such a confusion of ideas as clouds the text, and by consequence weakens the impression it would otherwise make upon our minds."

Here it is admitted, by Dr. Campbell, in his criticism upon these words, that they do refer to a *literal kingdom, and a literal government upon earth,* and the Lord of Hosts reigning literally in Jerusalem, and sitting literally upon the throne of his father David rebuilt there. The previous monarchies—namely, the Babylonian, the Medo-Persian, the Grecian, the Roman—spoken of in the second chapter of Daniel, were all literal monarchies. They had their literal existence upon earth, as their prophetic history foretold, and the providence of God has subsequently made manifest. In their day they had their literal ruler, or king, who occupied the throne; their literal government, or officers and legislation, by which their affairs were managed; their literal kingdom, or locality of reign, which, in each, was a clearly defined territory. All these were upon the earth, in visible form, and had their literal existence here. If then, four of the monarchies were literal, as is well known from history they were, and also from the still existing remains of the fourth, under the emblem of the ten toes, what can the presumption, or inference be, but that the fifth shall be of the same nature? If there is no change in the language, or style of prediction to warrant, by obvious meaning, or indubitable language, the expectation that there will be a change in the fulfilment of that portion of the prophecy yet to be fulfilled, it may, upon correct rules of interpretation, be expected, nay, confidently believed; and the whole dispensations of divine providence, proving the literal meaning of prophecy to be the true meaning, is God Almighty's own evidence, and proof of the soundness of this belief; that the fifth, the glorious monarchy yet to be set up at, and exist subsequent to, the destruction of the ten toes, will be also a literal monarchy upon the earth, and will have the king occupying the throne. But every reader knows there is no change of language clearly teaching, or even obscurely intimating, that prophecy yet unfulfilled shall not, like prophecy already fulfilled, have a literal fulfilment, but from henceforth, contrary to what has been uniform in past ages, it shall be spiritually fulfilled; and consequently we are shut up to a literal fulfilment, to the conclusion and belief that Messiah shall have a literal kingdom upon earth, and that he shall sit visibly and gloriously at the head of that monarchy upon the rebuilt throne of his father David.

All this seems very clearly taught by Daniel. The kingdom to be set up, destined to endure for ever, smites and destroys all that remains of the previous kingdoms, and takes possession of the very locality, as well as of the whole earth, which formed their kingdom. This then, must be a kingdom upon earth, a *literal* kingdom, like the preceding, though entirely different in its character, having nothing worldly, nothing sinful in its nature, nothing savouring of man, or the plans and policy of man, but everything from God, and of God ; a kingdom whose foundations are laid by infinite wisdom, in absolute righteousness. It is a kingdom not of this world, nor of the wisdom of this world, yet upon this earth ; for it comes down from God, having his own pure image impressed upon it, and his own holy and equitable legislation as the foundation and the rule of its entire government. It is divine in its origin, in its principles, in its laws of government. And to this literal kingdom, Daniel saw a literal king coming in the clouds of heaven to take possession thereof. He saw one like the Son of Man coming to the earth where he was, and where, also, appeared the Ancient of Days ; and to him was given dominion and glory, and a kingdom, that all peoples, nations, and languages, of course upon the earth, for these are nowhere else to be found, should serve him. Here then, we have a literal king, the Son of Man, the Lord Jesus Christ, who hung and died upon the cross, with this divinely secured, and most significant inscription over his head, "THE KING OF THE JEWS" —a literal government, He reigning in Jerusalem and in mount Zion, before, or in the presence of his ancients gloriously; he ruling literal subjects—all people, nations, and languages, a literal kingdom of the whole earth; which is the *literal* fulfilment of Gabriel's prediction to his mother—he shall sit upon the throne of his father David.

Surely, no reasonable objection can be adduced against the literal interpretation; and surely, no attempt ought to be made to adduce any, if such seem to be the revealed will and purpose of God. The creature has no right to say, that God means something else than the words used by the Spirit express, and that he has a right to say what that meaning is, and make out that to be something very different from that evidently conveyed by the language employed. Yet this right is assumed and boldly contended for; and in the exercise of it, many objections are brought against the literal fulfilment of prophecy foretelling Christ's personal and glorious reign upon the earth, after it has undergone important changes, making it fit for his residence. But let these objections be fairly and candidly examined in the light of Scripture, and the luminous exhibitions of divine providence, and in the absence of all prejudices and pre-embraced theories, and it is presumed that they will appear without much force, if not entirely groundless.

But if, objections are made to the literal interpretation, all these, after all, may not be a sufficient reason why it should be rejected. They may be groundless objections, and therefore without force; or they may be objections originating in our incapacity, fully to understand the subject in all its mysteries and details. And if we reject this view of Scripture, because there are some things which we cannot fully understand, we must also, to be consistent, reject many other statements and revelations which they make, and, among these, the spiritual or figurative interpretations. Objections, strong objections, can be brought against it; objections more numerous and powerful than can be brought against the literal interpretation. Indeed, there seems, every objection against it, inasmuch as it appears contrary to the whole analogy of Scripture, as well as to all the clear teachings of the Spirit of God. And were the soundness of the two views to be decided by the smallest number, and the least weighty objections which could be brought against each, then, beyond all controversy, the spiritual would be rejected as unsound, and the literal retained as orthodox.

If then, our interpretation of Scripture, respecting David and Messiah's throne, has been sound and correct, and our reasoning upon that interpretation legitimate, we are shut up to the conclusion, which is the doctrine clearly taught in the Scriptures, that David's throne, which has so long lain in ruins and been trampled under the feet of many centuries and the barbarous wanderers of the desert, and for which the eyes of the chosen race, the royal priesthood, have so long looked in vain, shall yet arise from its ruins, in glory far surpassing its former. The Lord himself shall be the builder, and he will make it a throne worthy of divine majesty and glory. It will be the throne of the whole earth. And the God-man, Christ Jesus, who died upon the cross, who slumbered in Joseph's tomb, but who is now enthroned on his father's right hand in the heavens, will come down, accompanied by all the thrones, dominions, principalities, and powers, and all the spirits of just men made perfect in paradise; and having raised their bodies from the grave, and greatly purged this earth of sin, and the effects of sin, he shall sit down in glory upon that resplendent and glorious throne, a redeemed creation rejoicing around him. That throne, rebuilt in matchless glory for the occupancy of the raised up seed of David according to the flesh, becomes, with its king, the centre and glorious attraction of the universe. From it, glory radiates forth unto all lands and all worlds. Around it, creation's holy ones assemble; before it, they bow and worship; and around it, their ever-swelling floods of praise perpetually roll, to the glory and honour of him who sits thereon, the King of Kings and the Lord of Lords: "the Lord God shall give unto him the *throne* of his Father David."

> "See Salem built, the labour of a God!
> Bright as the sun the sacred city shines;
> All kingdoms and all princes of the earth
> Flock to that light; the glory of all lands
> Flows into her; unbounded is her joy,
> And endless her increase."

Reader, will not that be a glorious throne, a throne pre-eminent in glory? And will not they be a blessed people who will dwell in that glory, and stand in the presence of Him from whom it all emanates? Ah, blessed they must be, supremely blessed, and they only! It is here, and here alone, where perfect glory and blessedness are to be enjoyed. And the momentous inquiry I would press upon your heart is this, simply this: When that throne is rebuilt, and the LORD the KING sits thereon, and the glorious, beatified hosts gather around it, will you have a place among this blessed number; will your voice be mingling with theirs in the ceaseless rapturous melody, the undying hallelujahs ever ascending; will you be standing with them before that throne, and casting your glorious crown in the presence of IMMANUEL, the I AM who occupies the seat of universal dominion; and will your eye with theirs be ever turned to him as your elder brother, to drink in from his abiding presence fulness of joy for evermore? Reader, pause; answer this question, for it is a question of utmost moment; it is the question of questions. Withdraw from the world, withdraw from business, from all the concerns of this life; suspend everything, till this great question is answered; for all compared with this is less than the small dust of the balance, *is nothing*. If you value riches, the possession and everlasting inheritance of the riches of righteousness depend upon the right solution of this question—the possession "of the inheritance incorruptible, undefiled, and that fadeth not away," the everlasting kingdom of God. Oh, upon the right solution of this question depends your everlasting life and happiness in the presence of the throne and its occupant! Your interest for eternity, vast in magnitude beyond all computation; your happiness for eternity; oh, your eternal life, and blessedness, and glory, depend upon the right solution of this question, upon your standing before that throne when rebuilt! Reader, will you then be among the number who shall stand in glory around that throne? Shall I meet you there? Shall God's redeemed people meet you there? Shall Christ see you there? And shall you for ever feel the blessedness of being there? The LORD the KING *waits* your answer.

CHAPTER II.

MESSIAH'S KINGDOM.

"He shall reign over the house of Jacob."—LUKE i. 33.

WE have seen that David had a literal throne, in his palace on mount Zion, in Jerusalem; and that he sat literally upon that throne, and reigned literally over the Jewish nation and people. He never had any other throne, nor any other kingdom, nor exercised any other government. This throne, then, was *the throne* promised to the Messiah, who was to be of David's seed. And though this throne of David has long ago tumbled into ruins, amidst the changes and convulsions of earth, the overturning of this world's kingdoms, yet the sure word of prophecy reveals and declares that it shall, at a set time, at an appointed season, be rebuilt, for the occupancy of the resurrection humanity—of the man-God, Christ Jesus. Prophecy does not speak of a throne which has had no previous existence, to be occupied by the raised up seed of David, namely, Jesus Christ, but only of *the throne* of David. If then it is admitted that Christ is to occupy a throne, according to the sure word of prophecy, it must be the literal throne of his father David. It will not do merely to affirm that the human heart is the throne here meant, and that Christ is to sit and reign spiritually there, until it is proved that David's throne in Jerusalem was the human heart; and that his reign was also a spiritual reign; and until it is shown how David, a literal man, could sit in the heart of men; and that he could sit in the heart of each individual of the entire Jewish nation at one and the same time. When that is done then, by the help of this wonderful new light poured upon us, we may be enabled to see or understand, in some measure, though of this we have doubts, how the raised up seed, the true humanity of Jesus Christ, may enter the bosom and sit in the heart of his people; how he may, in human nature, be in every heart of the vast multitude of his subjects, the number of whom shall be as the stars of the sky, as the dewdrops of the morning; and how the whole multitude of the risen saints, who are to sit with him upon his throne, shall, in their resurrection bodies, sit with him in every human heart in which he is to sit and reign when he occupies the throne of his father David.

As this, however, has not been done, and, as we presume, cannot be, we are constrained to hold the literal view presented in the word of God, and sustained by his providential fulfilment of prophecy, that

Christ shall sit in all his divine and kingly glory upon the rebuilt throne of his father David. And if he is to sit personally and literally upon that throne, so also is he to reign literally and visibly. Not only will he reign in the hearts of men, but he will reign visibly, as any other king reigns. This is the conclusion to which we were led by the grammatical meaning of prophecy, and by God's own interpretation, as given in his providence, in the literal fulfilment of prophecy, which hitherto has had its accomplishment.

If Christ is to occupy a literal throne, and be a literal king, and we think this is most clearly and certainly taught in Scripture, then he will and must have a literal kingdom, a literal territory, and people over which he must reign; and this is also clearly taught by the angel Gabriel, in his prophecy and promise to his virgin mother. Nor is this all; but in that same prophecy the kingdom, and the extent of Messiah's kingdom, is pointed out in these words: "He shall reign over the house of Jacob." And we propose now to glance for a little at the *locality* and *extent* of this kingdom.

It is predicted and affirmed by the angel Gabriel, that Jesus Christ, the Son of the Highest, who is to sit literally upon the rebuilt throne of his father David, shall reign over the house of Jacob. In order that we may form something like an accurate idea of the locality and extent of the kingdom described by the *house of Jacob*, we must take into consideration God's ancient promise and covenant with the patriarchs; the full extent of its meaning, and the subsequent descriptive predictions of the prophets, pointing out the far extending boundaries of that kingdom. We must look at it as it is set forth in Scripture from the first time it is mentioned to the last, and thus endeavour to see it in all its amplitude. And here, too, we must guard against the darkening influences of prepossessions and prejudices, and endeavour to see it in the clear unclouded light of revelation.

Jacob was the younger son of Isaac, and the grandson of Abraham. Now God gave by covenant to Abraham and his seed the whole land of Canaan, for an everlasting possession. The deed of gift, or covenant, is as follows: "The Lord said unto Abram, after that Lot was separated from him, Lift up now thine eyes, and look from the place where thou art, northward, and southward, and eastward, and westward, for *all the land* which thou seest to thee will I give it, and to thy seed for ever. And I will make thy seed as the dust of the earth; so that if a man can number the dust of the earth, then shall thy seed also be numbered. Arise, walk through the land in the length of it, and in the breadth of it, for I will give it unto thee" (Gen. xiii. 14–17). The land in which Abram was at this time, and which is here spoken of, was the land of Canaan. And while Abram, at the command of Jehovah, looked upon that land which lay before and around him, he did certainly believe that it was of that very territory that God spake, and that very territory which he in these words bequeathed to him by promise and covenant. How could he think otherwise, when God himself was directing his eye, his attention, and his faith to that very land, and in the most solemn manner, assuring him that he would give it to him and to his seed? He could never suppose, when God was commanding him to look upon that land, to walk over that land, and promising to give to him and his seed what he saw with the natural eye and trod upon, for an everlasting inheritance, that He all the while meant some region, or something undefined in heaven—something neither before his eyes nor under his feet, nor even upon the earth where he was.

Abram, pre-eminent for his faith, doubtless understanding and believing the words in their literal meaning; and knowing that he who had uttered the promise was fully able to perform it, "Said, Lord God, whereby shall I know that I shall inherit it?" that is, that I shall inherit *this land* where I now am, upon which I now look, and over which thou hast commanded me to walk. The Lord who had promised, knowing that Abram understood the promise, for if he had not He certainly would have corrected his mistake upon a subject of such vast moment, instantly condescended to give him a sign. He commanded him "to take a heifer, a goat, a ram, a turtle dove, and a young pigeon; and he took and divided them in the midst, and laid each piece over against the other; but the birds he divided not." This being done, it only remained for Abram to guard the carcasses from the fowls of heaven, until the time for the manifestation of the sign. "And it came to pass, that when the sun went down, and it was dark, behold a smoking furnace and a burning lamp that passed between those pieces. In the same day the Lord made a covenant with Abram, saying, *Unto thy seed have I given this land, from the river of Egypt unto the great river, the river Euphrates*" (Gen. xv.). Here then is the sign given by God, whereby Abram might know that he shall inherit the land, and the extent of the land partially defined.

Nor was this all, strong and conclusive and satisfactory as it may seem, that Abram and his seed should inherit that land; but when Abram was ninety and nine years old, and one year previous to the birth of the promised child, Isaac, that covenant, involving so many blessings, was renewed; Abram's name changed to Abraham; and another sign or token of the everlasting covenant, as it is called, was given, the token of circumcision. For thus saith the Lord, "This is my covenant which ye shall keep between me and you, and thy seed after thee: Every man child among you shall be circumcised; and ye shall circumcise the flesh of your foreskin; and it shall be *a token* of the covenant between me and you. He that is born in thy house, and he that is bought with thy money, must needs be circumcised; and my covenant shall be in *your flesh for an eaerlasting covenant."* This token or sign of the fulfilment of the everlasting covenant which God made with Abraham has been from that day, and still is in the flesh of every Jew, and will remain in their flesh as visible evidence of God's faithfulness, until the covenant of which it is the divine token or sign shall be fulfilled, according to the word of the Lord; until Abraham, on whom it was first performed, and all his seed with him, inherit the land of Canaan. And that is as sure a token to them, given by God himself, that they shall inherit that land; the very territory upon which Abraham, at the command of the Lord, looked; the land from the river of Egypt unto the great river, the river Euphrates, as the magnificent bow in the cloud is to us the divine token and testimony that the waters shall no more become a flood to destroy all flesh that is upon the face of the earth. The token of the one covenant as certainly secures its fulfilment as does the token of the other; and whatever may be the seeming difficulties in the way of its fulfilment, it ought to be remembered these are all nothing when the faithfulness and omnipotence of God are pledged to perform the work. Abraham and his descendants are to have the land, and doubtless, according to the fidelity of a covenant-keeping God, they *shall* have the land.

After Abraham had served his day and generation, and gone the way of all the earth, without obtaining the divinely-promised and covenanted land, or possessing as his own as much as whereon to set his foot, God appeared unto Isaac, and renewed the precious everlasting covenant made with his father to him. The covenant-making God to Abraham now becomes the covenant-making God to Isaac. The Lord appeared unto Isaac, and said, "Go not down into Egypt; dwell in the land which I shall tell thee of. Sojourn in this land, and I will be with thee, and will bless thee, for unto thee and unto thy seed I will give all these countries; and I will perform the oath which I sware unto thy father Abraham; and I will make thy seed to multiply as the stars of heaven, and will give unto thy seed *all these countries;* and in thy seed shall all nations of the earth be blessed" (Gen. xxvi. 2–4). The covenant here made with Isaac is evidently the very same as that made with his father Abraham; and it must appear manifest to every reader that the thing covenanted is one and the same, the land of Canaan. And in this covenant too the Lord assures Isaac, that though his father Abraham was dead yet he would perform the oath which he had sworn, or fulfil the covenant which he had made with him; thereby distinctly intimating that death could not break this covenant, nor the grave cut Abraham off from possessing the land of Canaan; for though he had died, and gone down to the depths of the grave, yet God, true to his covenant and his oath, would restore him to life, and bring him up out of the grave, and give him that land. And this assurance concerning his deceased father

Abraham, was also the assurance to him, that though he should die before possessing that land, yet he would by God be raised up out of the grave, to inherit it with his father and his seed for ever. It was to be theirs by an everlasting covenant for an everlasting possession, and if they had possessed it only during their natural life, the terms of the covenant would in no respect have been fulfilled. In order to the complete fulfilment of these it is necessary, as we shall hereafter see, that Abraham, with his deceased descendants, should be brought up out of the grave to inherit that land.

God Almighty renewed this covenant upon a more extensive scale to Jacob. When he was fleeing from that very land, in obedience to his mother's fears, lest his enraged brother should slay him, because he had obtained his father's blessing which belonged to Esau by birthright; and, in obedience to his father's commands, that he should not take a wife of the daughters of Canaan, Isaac poured out his blessing upon his son, strongly expressive of his faith in what the Lord God had spoken : "God Almighty bless thee, and give thee the blessing of Abraham, to thee, and to thy seed with thee, that thou mayest inherit *the land* wherein thou art a stranger, which God gave unto Abraham" (Gen. xxviii. 4). The language here used by Isaac would seem almost to imply that Abraham did actually possess the land, whereas it was his only by promise and covenant, and not as yet his by possession. But so strong was his faith in the faithfulness of God, that he speaks of the thing yet to be done as if it were already done.

Before Jacob had travelled beyond the land of Canaan, the land of covenant; before the sun had arisen invoking him with cheering beams to prosecute his second day's journey to a land of safety, much more than a paternal blessing had been vouchsafed to him; he had received more to comfort his heart and sustain his soul than his earthly father, great and pious as he might be, had to bestow, even upon a favourite son. The God of Abraham and Isaac appeared to him, giving him ample assurance that he was also his God. For while the stones which he gathered after the sun had gone down were his pillow, the earth his bed, and the far spreading star-spangled sky his curtain, he, from whom the twelve tribes of Israel were appointed to spring, received, upon his solitary angel-guarded couch, the promise that *all that land*, the land wherein he lay, which was the land of Canaan, should be theirs. For thus said the Lord, from the top of the ladder where he stood, "I am the Lord God of Abraham, thy father; and the God of Isaac; the land wherein thou liest to thee will I give it, and to thy seed; and thy seed shall be as the dust of the earth, and thou shalt spread abroad to the west, and to the east, and to the north, and to the south; and in thee, and in thy seed, shall all the families of the earth be blessed" (Gen. xxviii. 13, 14).

Jacob, or Israel, as he was afterwards called, most firmly believed all this, though the promise had not been fulfilled either to his father or grandfather, though neither of them had possessed or inherited the land. He believed it all because he had it from the lips of Jehovah, who cannot lie, and who will not deceive; and hence he charged his sons, and even made his beloved Joseph swear, that he would not bury him in the land of Egypt, the land of the heathen, believing that he had to die before he could inherit the land of promise; but carry him into the land of Canaan, to the burying-place of his fathers, in the land given to them and him, and to his children, by God, in an everlasting covenant. And Joseph also took an oath from the children of Israel, binding them to do the same thing for him, to carry him into Canaan and bury him there. And the reason of all this was, because he and all that people believed the word and covenant of God making that land theirs; and because they believed, according to these, the time would come when it would be theirs by actual and everlasting possession, when they would inherit it as God's free and peculiar gift to them.

This promise and covenant of the faithful God have not yet been fulfilled, but are waiting the advent of "the times which the Father hath put in his own power" for their literal fulfilment. They were not fulfilled at the return of Israel from their long oppressive Egyptian bondage, for the patriarchs with whom they were made, and their offspring who died in that land of servitude, and during their punitive journeyings in the wilderness, were not with those privileged individuals whom Joshua led over Jordan's divided stream ; nor did they with them take possession of the land. When they crossed Jordan, and joyfully entered Canaan, Abraham, Isaac, and Jacob were slumbering in the grave, "prisoners of hope," waiting for God to call and they will answer him—arise and take possession of the land. Nor is this all, but the people who by miracle after miracle were led into that land did not, according to the tenor of promise and covenant, take possession of it; nor have they inherited it for ever ; nor is it in the possession of their descendants in the present day, though they are to possess it for ever; and consequently this covenant and promise have not yet been fulfilled to these men, highly favoured and greatly beloved of God; yet no doubt can be entertained of their fulfilment to the very letter, for the God who made them is faithful to all his engagements. And that God will fulfil his covenant to these men and their seed, Stephen argued clearly and conclusively, in the seventh chapter of the Acts of the Apostles. "For," says he, "then came he (Abraham) out of the land of the Chaldeans, and dwelt in Charran; and from thence, when his father was dead, he removed him into the land wherein ye now dwell. And he gave him none inheritance in it, no, not so much as to set his foot on; *yet he promised that he would give it to him for a possession, and to his seed after him*, when as yet he had no child." That land Abraham as yet never had for an inheritance, but according to this it shall be his ; and the fact of his descendants possessing it temporarily at the time when Stephen uttered these words was another divine evidence of the fulfilment of this covenant.

That the covenant and promise were made with Abraham, that he and his posterity should possess, and for ever inherit the land of Canaan, cannot be denied. It is equally true that they have not as yet inherited the land according to covenant and promise ; but as God who has promised to give them this land is a God of truth, who will certainly fulfil all his promises, it follows, as a matter equally certain, that they shall possess and inherit the land. This they must, this they shall do, unless God proves faithless to his solemn engagements. But this is an alternative too repugnant to be entertained for a single moment. As no good reason exists or can exist, as no insurmountable obstacle stands in the way or can stand in the way, why God should not fulfil this covenant with Abraham and his seed, the obvious and certain conclusion is, he will do it. The preparations have been advancing since the day the covenant was made ; they are going forward now, and when they have been completed, the divinely chosen and appointed heirs will enter upon their possession.

But before this everlasting covenant, so full of great

and precious blessings, can be fulfilled, before Abraham, Isaac, and Jacob, and their descendants, can inherit *the land*, theirs by divine gift and covenant, theirs by heavenly deed, it is evident they must be raised up out of their graves and restored to life; and those scattered to the four winds of heaven in the retributive justice of God, in answer to the fearful invocation of the guilt of the crucifixion of the Son of God being upon their heads, when they said, "His blood be upon us and our children," must be gathered. And all this, marvellous as it may seem, and incredible withal, even to many who are professedly diligent students of the word of God, according to the glorious predictions contained in the thirty-seventh chapter of Ezekiel, shall be done. And to the fulfilment of that covenant, as presented in that chapter, it may be important to look.

While Ezekiel sat, a grief-stricken captive, far from Shiloh's hallowed brook, which flowed fast by the oracle of God, on Chebar's dismal heathen banks, the hand of the Lord God came upon him, and filled him with the Spirit's influence, with prophetic inspiration. Under these strong, mighty influences and supernatural agency he was carried out into a valley where was scattered, in wild and warlike confusion, as if the wreck of many battles, and piled up in seeming disorder, very many, vast heaps of human bones. As he walked around and gazed upon these remains of the dead which had lived and acted in the busy scenes of men, and performed their part on the stage of time, he saw that all vital moisture had departed from them, and that in death they were very dry. Every vestige of life had fled, and no germ awakening the hope, or prognosticating their return to life, could be seen in them. To nature, and to reason's eye, they seemed the irreclaimable trophies of death.

While the prophet's eye rested upon them, and he was musing, in sadness and sorrow, upon their dryness, the inquiry of the Lord fell upon his ear, "Son of man, can these bones live?" The question he felt far too difficult for him to answer. He shrank from hazarding an opinion; declared such knowledge too high for him; and threw back the responsibility of saying whether these dry bones could live upon the Lord who had proposed it, "O Lord God, thou knowest."

Upon this he was commanded to prophesy upon these dry bones, and invoke them to hear the word of the Lord; and tell them that the Lord would cause breath to enter into them; that he would lay sinews, flesh, and skin upon them; make them live and know that he is the Lord. In prompt and profound obedience to this high and strange behest of heaven, the prophet proceeded to the work; "For," says he, "so I prophesied as I was commanded; and as I prophesied there was a noise, and behold a shaking, and the bones came together, bone to his bone." In the prophet's voice there seemed the omnipotence of God; for as it rolled over that valley in which were piled up heaps of dry bones, dismal for its silence, awful for its stillness and accumulated tokens of death, there burst forth a noise. Influences new, mighty, and portentous seemed to be in operation; a mighty principle of life seemed at work in the realms and citadel of death. The dried remains of mortality felt its power, and began to shake under its influences. It entered these bones strangely, miraculously, communicating to them the power of action and the power of recognition, enabling them to move, and, amidst the confused heaps, unerringly to recognise their fellows, and to come together to a second and everlasting union. Now was heard the thrilling rattling, now was seen the wonderful stirring of the very dry bones, in strange commotion, each with apparent eagerness seeking his fellow from among the vast multitude, and when found rushing together with impetuous fondness, like ardent lovers, who had long been separated. "Bone came to his fellow bone," till each and all had found their previous companion, their previous place, till every human skeleton was perfect. And while the prophet gazed upon these bones, no longer in confused heaps but regularly arranged in their places, as they had been in the days of life, articulated skeletons, lo, the sinews came and bound them all together; bone was again knit to bone, with sinews stronger than before, with sinews immortal, and flesh came upon them, and skin covered them. And now, to the prophet's eye, the valley was full, not of dry human bones, but full of perfect human forms. There they lay, all complete—fresh, beautiful, lovely—like so many hushed in sleep, enjoying refreshing repose, waiting in their slumbers for the bright dawning of the cloudless morn, to enter upon the activities of existence. But fresh and beautiful though they looked, clothed in their new flesh and skin, and blushing in more than pristine loveliness, yet there was no life in them.

Again the voice of the Lord fell upon Ezekiel's ear, saying, "Prophesy unto the wind, and say unto the wind, Thus saith the Lord God, Come from the four winds, O breath, and breathe upon these slain, that they may live." The word here translated breath, wind, signifies wind, breath, soul, spirit of man. Each of these is essential to the life of the body, and each of these—not only in the Bible, but in common phraseology—is frequently used as expressive of life. Since the original word has such a variety of shades of meaning, the particular shade must be determined by the sense of the passage in which it occurs.

Now the word wind here doubtless signifies the soul or spirit of man. I believe all interpreters agree in this. The four winds must signify the four cardinal points whence the wind blows. In this sense this expression is used in Scripture. It denotes then far remote and invisible places, places not seen, not explored by mortal eye. It has been remarked, that breath has the same meaning as wind: it signifies spirit, soul of man, as is manifest from the tenth verse, where it is said that breath or soul entered into them; that is to say, that the spirits in the remote places serving God, at the divine call, returned and entered into the reconstructed or resurrection body. Now, if this interpretation be correct, then, stripped of all shades of Hebrew fertility of language, and rendered in plain English, it would read thus: "Then said he to me, Prophesy to the souls or spirits (that is, to the souls or spirits of these lifeless bodies), prophesy, son of man, and say to the spirits or souls, Thus saith the Lord God, Come from the north, south, east, and west, come from the remote and invisible places where ye now dwell, O souls, and enter into these slain, that they may live. So I prophesied as he commanded me, and the souls came into them, and they lived, and stood up upon their feet, an exceeding great army." The bones, now clothed with flesh and skin, the bodies which lay in beautiful perfection, yet lifeless, were again repossessed by the revoked soul, and reanimated by the living principle, stood up, an exceeding great and glorious army—beautiful, resplendent in the divine freshness of their young resurrection.

Hitherto the prophetic style has been kept up, as if all in this vision were literal; the bones literal, the sinews, flesh, skin, souls, all literal, and the souls entering into these bodies, and their rising and standing up, literal. This has been done, not in ignorance that all this has been allegorized, and that the allegorizing has led to very different explanations. Some of these allegorizers have said that the dry bones symbolized the Jews in Babylonish captivity ; that the publication of Cyrus on behalf of the Jews was the shaking of the bones ; that the edict published by Darius, in the second year of his reign, removing impediments out of the way, was the clothing of these bones with flesh ; and that the mission of Nehemiah, with orders from Artaxerxes to complete the building of the temple, was the entering of life into them. And surely, beyond all controversy, this is allegorical enough ; so highly allegorical that its extravagant absurdities are its own refutation. A people in captivity symbolized by dry bones ! Edicts of men in authority, by sinews, flesh, and skin ! And a command to build the temple and city, by spirits entering into human bodies ! Surely this is an interpretation so palpably erroneous, that it is unnecessary to enter into any argumentation to refute it. This is a manner and mystic style of which we have no authenticated instance of the Holy Spirit speaking to the children of men. And besides all this, the Spirit's own interpretation of the vision refutes it, as we shall afterwards see.

Some have made this vision symbolical of Israel's conversion to Christianity. To this view there are also strong objections. It makes dry bones a symbol of unbelieving Jews ; flesh and skin a symbol of—it is difficult to say what, holiness, or something else ; breath entering into them, conversion or regeneration. Others, again, contend that this is a prophecy concerning the conversion of the heathen ; and that when the gospel is preached in every land, and all the heathen converted by its instrumentality, then this prediction will be fulfilled. We are most certain this cannot be the meaning of the prophecy. These dry bones are not symbolic of the heathen, for the Holy Ghost declares, " these bones are the whole house of Israel." The term Israel here is a distinctive name, and denotes only the descendants of Israel, the seed of Abraham, the Jews. Israel is never once used in Scripture to denote the heathen or Gentile nations, but uniformly the children of Abraham, the peculiar, the chosen, the covenant people of God. Israel therefore cannot mean the heathen here, as it never does anywhere, and consequently their conversion is not foretold in the passage ; but, on the contrary, the resurrection of Abraham and his descendants.

Now it does appear that there is no symbol, no figure, in the vision of the valley of dry bones. All is literal, and ought to be understood just as it reads, and according to the common acceptation of language. If this is not a description of a literal resurrection, then we have not a literal resurrection described in the Bible. We have here the great and grand rudimental parts of the human body, and these too accurately and beautifully anatomically arranged. We have the bones, and then the sinews or tendons, which strongly bind together and partially cover these bones, and then we have the flesh attached to these sinews and covering them ; and then we have the skin inwrapping all in its delicate and beautiful texture, and, to complete the living being, the spirit is revoked from the invisible place of residence, and by the power of God made to enter the newly reconstructed body, and then what had been lifeless, dead, stand up an army of living human beings. The literality of this passage is inadvertently admitted by these allegorizers ; for when they come to speak of a literal resurrection they freely use this passage as referring to that event and describing it. Now one thing is certain, it cannot have both an allegorical and literal interpretation. And when it is obviously literal, and the literal meaning so obvious, why should there be any effort to mystify it by allegorizing ?

But this is not all ; the Holy Ghost interprets it literally, and the whole of the Scriptures, referring to God's covenant with Abraham and his seed, interpret it literally. And consequently this is one of the strong passages teaching that God's covenant with that people, which has never yet been fulfilled, *shall* be fulfilled, and that all those who died in the faith of inheriting the land of covenant and promise *shall* yet possess it.

Concerning these bones the Holy Ghost declares they are the whole house of Israel, or Jacob. Israel is the name which the angel gave to Jacob after having wrestled all night with him at Mahanaim. It signifies a prince of God. It is sometimes used to denote Jacob, the person to whom it was originally given ;

and very frequently, as every reader of the Bible knows, it denotes the descendants of Jacob ; and sometimes all the tribes of Israel, or the whole house of Jacob—Abraham and his descendants. And the expression, "these bones are the whole house of Israel," is doubtless to be understood in its most extensive signification, as meaning all the children of Jacob or Israel—all the descendants of Abraham, *according to the faith.* Not all his natural posterity, but all his natural *believing* posterity ; for the covenant was not made with the children according to the flesh merely, *but with the children according to the flesh and the faith.* By the expression, then, "these bones are the whole house of Israel," we are to understand the whole *believing* house of Israel, who have died and gone down to the chambers of the dead. All their bones were exhibited to Ezekiel in vision ; and not only theirs, but all who have died in the faith since the time of the vision; and not only they, but all of Abraham's believing seed who shall yet die before the glorious resurrection of the vision shall be realized. These dry bones, then, are the literal bones of all Abraham's *believing children,* according to the interpretation of the Holy Ghost ; and these bones are to be restored to life, that they may inherit the promised land, and that God's ancient and never-forgotten covenant made with Abraham, renewed to Isaac and Jacob, and clearly referred to by the angel Gabriel, when announcing the conception of the Messiah to his virgin mother, may be fulfilled.

The angel Gabriel, in his announcement to Mary, evidently quotes from the prophet Ezekiel. Ezekiel says these bones are the whole *house of Israel;* Gabriel says he shall reign over the *house of Jacob.* Israel and Jacob are but different names of the same person; and if the bones in the valley of Ezekiel's vision are the whole house, or representatives of the whole house of Israel or Jacob, then when the promise made by the angel to Mary is fulfilled, Jesus, or the Son of the Highest, shall reign over these bones; for these bones are the whole house of Israel or Jacob.

The prophet represents them in the state in which he saw them as giving utterance to their despondency in these words, "Behold, they say, our bones are dried, and our hope is lost; we are cut off for our parts." This may be viewed as the language of despair, involving an unanswerable argument that God's covenant with them would never be fulfilled—they would never inherit the land of Canaan. It is as if these lifeless things were endued with speech only to tell and argue their dismal despair. "Our bones are dried," so thoroughly dried, that there is no living moisture in them, and their dryness is the unanswerable argument that they cannot live. But in response to this, true, and powerful, and conclusive as it may seem, Jehovah replies, "*You shall live.*"

"Our hope is lost." What are we to understand by this expression? What is the hope of Israel, said to be lost? Hope is the expectation of future good: but in Scripture it is frequently used for the thing hoped for, and that is doubtless the meaning of the term hope here. According to this, then, the thing hoped for is lost. Now what was the thing hoped for by Israel? It is doubtless the land given by God in covenant to Abraham, Isaac, and Jacob; the land in which they, and their Shiloh at their head, are to dwell in peace, plenty, happiness, and glory, exalted above, and reigning over all other nations. That this was the hope of Israel Paul has placed beyond the possibility of a doubt, in his defence before king Agrippa, when he says, "I stand and am judged for *the hope of the promise* made of God unto our fathers; unto which promise our twelve tribes, serving God day and night, expect to come. *For which hope's sake*, king Agrippa, I am accused of the Jews." The same truth is clearly taught in the explanation which he gave to the Jews in Rome, for being in the custody of a Roman soldier, when he said, "For the HOPE OF ISRAEL am I bound with this chain." God promised to the fathers and their seed the land of Canaan for an everlasting possession; this land, in consequence of this promise, became *the hope* of that whole people or nation. That inheritance was the thing hoped for by Abraham and all his descendants, and that is *the hope* divinely begotten in the heart of every Jew; and wherever you find one of Abraham's scattered children, you find this *hope* occupying a pre-eminent place in his bosom, and his eye and affections ever turning to that land of promise and of hope.

Now the dry bones are represented as saying "our *hope* is lost;" the inheritance and all its concomitant blessings promised to our fathers are lost to us; we are dead and dried, and can never inherit that land, which is thy land, O Immanuel. But the spirit of prophecy contradicts the despondency; the Lord God says, your hope is not lost, your promised inheritance not lost, it shall yet be yours, for I, by my mighty power, will restore life to your dry bones, will bring you up out of your graves; "I will bring you *into the land of Israel; I will place you in your own land.*" Though you be dead, and your bones dry, yet your hope, your inheritance, is not lost. I will restore you to life, and bring you into that land I have covenanted to give you. You shall dwell in that land, and my Beloved shall be king over you all.

It is added farther, "We are cut off for our parts." This might have been rendered, we are dead or destroyed from our parts; that is, we are dead, and consequently cut off from the land of promise to our fathers, for this is what is meant by parts. It signifies rest, habitation, possession, inheritance. Being dead they feel they were cut off from that inheritance, and that the land of Israel was not to be theirs. But this was not so; God's purpose and covenant were yet to be fulfilled; and though they were dead, yet in order to the fulfilment of that covenant they would be raised to life, brought up out of their graves, and brought into their own land; and then they would know and feel that they were not cut off from their parts.

It may be proper to notice in passing that "*the hope of Israel*," or the thing promised in the Abrahamic covenant, is the one great, grand, and glorious hope of the gospel. "*The hope*," or the thing promised in the Abrahamic covenant and the gospel, are not different, but the same. There is not one hope to the believing Jew and another to the believing Gentile; but one *hope*, common to both; for by faith the Gentile becomes the spiritual seed of Abraham, and an heir of the same promise, or inheritance, namely, *the promised land, the kingdom of God and Shiloh.* This is clearly the doctrine of Paul, in his Epistle to the Galatians, when he says, "Ye are all the children of God by faith in Christ Jesus. For as many of you as have been baptized into Christ have put on Christ. There is neither Jew nor Greek, there is neither bond nor free, there is neither male nor female; for ye are all one in Christ Jesus. *And if ye be Christ's then are ye Abraham's seed and heirs, according to the promise.*" He teaches precisely the same doctrine when he tells us that Abraham, Isaac, Jacob, the fathers, and the multitude of the Old Testament saints, the more conspicuous of whom he mentions in the eleventh chapter of his Epistle to the Hebrews—the great cloud of witnesses—"all died in the faith," not having received the promises, that is the thing contained in the promises, which is the land of Canaan, the hope of Israel. And the reason of their not attaining this he assigns—" that they," the fathers, " without us," their remote believing descendants, and the believing Gentiles, " might not be made perfect." The fathers were not the only individuals who were to inherit that land ; there were other heirs, heirs of the seed of Abraham according to the flesh, and Gentile heirs of the seed of Abraham according to the faith ; and consequently the Fathers, with whom the covenant was made, could not inherit the thing bequeathed in the covenant until all the heirs were ready and prepared to enter upon the inheritance with them ; they without us who had to live in these remote ages of the world and Christianity " could not be made perfect."

They are not perfect now, their spirits are only waiting and their flesh resting, in the hope of that coming perfection. They may be, and doubtless are, shining in glory and rejoicing in happiness in paradise; but whatever may be their situation there, it is distinctly admitted by Paul that they are not perfect. Their spirits may be perfect in holiness, but as redeemed human beings they are not perfect, neither have they as yet entered upon their inheritance. And this perfection they cannot attain until their bodies arise from the grave ; neither can they possess *the inheritance*, *the hope*, until they arise. When they are raised up out of their graves, their bodies fashioned like unto Christ's glorious body, then will they be made perfect, then will they be made like God, and enter upon the possession of their inheritance. But they have not thus been made perfect, neither are they to be without us, and all subsequent believers under the gospel dispensation, until all whom the Father has given to the Son be born and brought to the faith ; for all believers in all ages have to be made perfect, and enter upon the inheritance at the same time, the time of the first resurrection. Then will be the time of believing Israel, believing Jew, and Gentile, being made perfect, and entering upon the possession of their hope, the land of Israel.

The hope of the Abrahamic covenant, then, and the hope of the gospel is the same ; or the thing promised to Abraham and his believing children in the covenant, and the thing promised to believing Gentiles in the gospel, is the same. The thing promised is the land of Judea, Immanuel's land, the kingdom of God, the kingdom of the Father, the inheritance incorruptible, undefiled, and that fadeth not away. This is the kingdom which Abraham, Isaac, and Jacob, when the covenant with them and Christ their seed is fulfilled—and it is the kingdom too which the believing, the saved Gentiles, who through faith become heirs of the promise—are to inherit when they come from the four winds of heaven, and sit down with these fathers "*in the kingdom.*" This is clearly the teaching of the Bible, and especially is it the teaching of the gospel of the Son of God. And if this Abrahamic covenant, which is in reality the very foundation of the gospel, be not understood, then the gospel, apart from that covenant, cannot be understood; if the hope of the covenant is not understood, the hope of the gospel cannot be understood, for they are not only inseparably connected, they are one. Neither can it be understood how believers of the gospel can be Abraham's seed, "and with him heirs according to the promise."

But to return. We have seen that all Abraham's seed slumbering in the grave, which are the house of Jacob, are to be raised up out of their graves and brought into the land of Canaan, the land of covenant and promise. Simultaneous with the fulfilment of this glorious prediction, will be the fulfilment of that in the subsequent part of the chapter referring to the Jews then living upon the earth. The Jews living upon the earth at that time as they are now, in a state of dispersion, tribe separated from tribe, and all distinctions so thoroughly lost, that no man can tell from whom he has descended—these people scattered to the winds of heaven, and dwelling in every land, and among every people, oppressed, persecuted by all—these people, the people of the covenant, long and miraculously kept separate from the heathen among whom they have lived, are to be gathered and brought back into their own land—brought back to their own city Jerusalem, which is to be rebuilt, when "the times of the Gentiles are fulfilled," and to their much loved and ever remembered "Zion with songs and everlasting joy upon their heads," and to their long looked for Shiloh, "to whom the gathering of the people shall be," for they too are a part of the house of Jacob. "Thus saith the Lord God, Behold I will take the children of Israel from among the heathen, whither they be gone, and I will gather them on every side, and bring them into *their own land:* and I will make them one nation in the land upon the mountains of Israel: and one king shall be king to them all; and they shall be no more two nations, neither shall they be divided into two kingdoms any more at all: neither shall they defile themselves any more with their idols, nor with their detestable things, nor any of their transgressions: but I will save them out of all their dwelling-places wherein they have sinned, and will cleanse them; so that they be my people, and I will be their God. And David my servant shall be king over them all: and they shall have one shepherd: they shall also walk in my judgments, and observe my statutes, and do them. And they shall dwell *in the land that I have given to Jacob* my servant, wherein your fathers have dwelt: and they shall dwell therein, even they and their children, and their children's children for ever; and my servant David shall be their prince for ever. Moreover, I will make a covenant of peace with them: it shall be an everlasting covenant with them: and I will *place* them, and multiply them, and will set my sanctuary in the midst of them for evermore. My tabernacle also shall be with them: yea I will be their God, and they shall be my people. And the heathen," or Gentiles, "shall know that I the Lord do sanctify Israel, when my sanctuary shall be in the midst of them for evermore." (Ezek. xxxvii. 21–28.)

Now in all this it is clearly and plainly taught, that dispersed Israel, or Jacob, shall be gathered from the lands, whither God in his anger has driven them, into their own land. Nor is this taught only in the prophecy which we have just quoted; but in many other prophecies of which the following may serve as a specimen. The whole of the forty-ninth chapter of Isaiah teaches strongly and clearly this truth:—represents Israel or Jacob, as gathered by the Lord out of all nations: their enemies utterly destroyed; the heavens singing, the earth rejoicing over their return to Zion; and concludes by declaring that "all flesh shall know that the Lord is their Saviour and Redeemer, the mighty one of Jacob"—the king to reign over the house of Jacob. And when speaking of the great and glorious work of Israel's gathering, as being already accomplished, and they dwelling safely in their own inheritance: "The Sun shall be no more thy light by day: neither for brightness shall the moon give light unto thee: but the Lord shall be unto thee an everlasting light, and thy God thy glory. Thy sun shall no more go down: neither shall thy moon withdraw itself: for the Lord shall be thine everlasting light, and the days of thy mourning shall be ended. Thy people shall be all righteous: they shall inherit the land for ever, the branch of my planting, the work of my hands, that I may be glorified. A little one shall become a thousand, and a small one a strong nation: I the Lord will hasten it in his time" (Isa. lx. 19–22). Jeremiah says, "Behold the days come, saith the Lord, that I will raise unto David a righteous Branch, and a king shall reign and prosper, and shall execute judgment, and justice on the earth. In his days Judah shall be saved, and Israel shall dwell safely; and this is his name whereby he shall be called, THE LORD OUR RIGHTEOUSNESS. Therefore, behold, the days come, saith the Lord, that they shall no more say, the Lord liveth which brought up the children of Israel out of the land of Egypt: but the Lord liveth which brought up, and which led the seed of the house of Israel, out of the north country, and from all countries whither I have driven them; and they shall dwell in their own land" (chap. xxiii. 5–8). And again, "Behold, I will gather them out of all countries whither I have driven them in mine anger, and in my fury, and in great wrath; and I will bring them again into this place, and I will cause them to dwell safely; and they shall be my people, and I will be their God. And I will give them one heart, and one way, that they may fear me for ever, for the good of them, and of their children after them: and I will make an everlasting covenant with them, that I will not turn away from them, to do them good; but I will put my fear in their hearts, that they shall not depart from me. Yea, I will rejoice over them to do them good, and I will plant them in this land assuredly with my whole heart, and with my whole soul" (chap. xxxii. 37–41). So in the following chapter (v. 7–14), "And I will cause the captivity of Judah, and the captivity of Israel to return, and will build them, as at the first. And I will cleanse them from all their iniquity, whereby they have sinned, and whereby they have transgressed against me. And it shall be to me a name of joy, a praise and an honour before all the nations of the earth, which shall hear all the good that I do unto them: and they shall fear and tremble for all the goodness, and all the prosperity, that I procure unto it. Thus saith the Lord, again there shall be heard in this place, which ye say shall be desolate without man, and without beast, even in the cities of Judah, and in the streets of Jerusalem, that are desolate, without man, and without inhabitant, and without beast, the voice of joy, and the voice of gladness, the voice of the bridegroom, and the voice of the bride; the voice of them that shall say, praise the LORD of hosts: for the Lord is good; for his mercy endureth for ever: and of them that shall bring the sacrifice of praise into the house of the LORD. Thus saith the LORD of hosts, again in this place, which is desolate, without man, and without beast, and in all the cities thereof, shall be an habitation of shepherds causing their flocks to lie down. In the cities of the mountains, in the cities of the vale, and in the cities of the south, and in the land of Benjamin, and in the places about Jerusalem, and in the cities of Judah, shall the flocks pass again under the hand of him that telleth them, saith the Lord. Behold the days come, saith the Lord, that I will perform that good thing which I have promised unto the house of Israel, and to the house of Judah." Other prophecies from Ezekiel might be quoted, but one shall suffice. "For I will take you from among the heathen, and gather you out of all countries, and will bring you into *your own land.* Then will I sprinkle clean water upou you, and ye shall be clean : from all your filthiness, and from all your idols will I cleanse you. A new heart also will I give you, and a new spirit will I put within you ; and I will take away the stony heart out of your flesh, and I will give you a heart of flesh. And I will put my spirit within you, and cause you to walk in my statutes, and ye shall keep my judgments and do them. And ye shall dwell in the land I gave to your fathers ; and ye shall be my people, and I will be your God. I will also save you from all your uncleannesses ; and I will call for the corn, and will increase it, and lay no famine upon you. And I will multiply the fruit of the tree, and the increase of the field, that ye shall receive no more reproach of famine among the heathen." (Ezek. xxxvi. 24–30.)

The minor prophets teach with equal clearness the same glorious truth, for thus it is written, in Amos ix. 11–15 : "In that day will I raise up the tabernacle of David that is fallen, and close up the breaches thereof: and I will raise up his ruins, and I will build it as in the days of old : that they may possess the remnant of

Edom, and of all the heathen, which are called by my name, saith the Lord, that doeth this. Behold the days come, saith the Lord, that the plowman shall overtake the reapers, and the treader of grapes him that soweth seed: and the mountains shall drop sweet wine and all the hills shall melt. And I will bring again the captivity of my people of Israel, and they shall build the waste cities, and inhabit them; and they shall plant vineyards, and drink the wine thereof; they shall also make gardens, and eat the fruit of them. And I will plant them upon their land, and they shall no more be pulled up out of their land, which I have given them, saith the Lord thy God." Zephaniah says, "Behold, at that time I will undo all that afflict thee; and I will save her that halteth, and gather her that was driven out; and I will get them praise and fame in every land where they have been put to shame. At that time will I bring you again, even in the time that I gather you; for I will make you a name and a praise among all the people of the earth, when I turn back your captivity before your eyes, saith the Lord" (chap. iii. 19, 20). And again, "Thus saith the Lord, I am returned unto Zion, and will dwell in the midst of Jerusalem; and Jerusalem shall be called a city of truth, and the mountain of the Lord of hosts, the holy mountain. Thus saith the Lord of hosts, There shall yet old men and old women dwell in the streets of Jerusalem, and every man with his staff in his hand for very age. And the streets of the city shall be full of boys and girls playing in the streets thereof. Thus saith the Lord of hosts, If it be marvellous in the eyes of the remnant of this people in these days, should it also be marvellous in mine eyes? saith the Lord of hosts. Thus saith the Lord of hosts, Behold, I will save my people from the east country, and from the west country; and I will bring them, and they shall dwell in the midst of Jerusalem; and they shall be my people, and I will be their God, in truth and in righteousness" (Zech. viii. 3–8).

Now surely these prophetic portions of God's word do most clearly and distinctly teach that dead Israel, represented by the dry bones, shall be restored to life; shall be brought up out of their graves, and brought into their own land; and that dispersed, wandering, bleeding, God-afflicted Israel, shall be gathered from the four winds of heaven and brought into that same land of covenant and promise. When these prophetic declarations, almost universally admitted to be yet unfulfilled, are fulfilled; when all these people are gathered into the land of Israel, they will form the house of Israel, or, according to the angel Gabriel, the house of Jacob, and David, the servant of God the Father, "will be king over them all;" or he shall reign over them all as the house of Jacob.

The word David, the name generally given to the sweet singer of Israel, the son of Jesse, does not, in the prophecy under consideration, refer to that individual. The word David signifies, Beloved, my Beloved; and here, as elsewhere, denotes or means Jesus Christ, as is admitted by commentators. And the precious truth taught is, that he, the Father's Beloved, is to reign over the united nation of Israel, signified by the house of Jacob gathered into their own land; and consequently, in this respect, the territorial extent of Messiah's kingdom will be the whole land of Israel, or Canaan, " a large land."

What will be the actual number of the house of Jacob, when fully gathered from the grave and the lands of their dispersion, and brought by the mighty hand and the glorious power of the God of the covenant, it is impossible to say, calculate, or even in any degree conjecture. But when we think on the resurrection, and changed glorified saints, which will be a multitude which no man can number, and the mortal saints converted at that period, and their ever increasing numbers, we must see and feel persuaded that the house of Jacob, the heirs of the land, the subjects of Messiah, will form a multitude great and glorious beyond all computation. Then will the children of the covenant, the seed of Abraham, of Jacob, be as the stars of the sky, as the sand upon the sea-shore; and if these cannot be numbered, neither can the gathered house of Jacob, neither can the subjects of Prince Messiah's kingdom. And whatever may be the number of the subjects of this divine and glorious kingdom at its commencement, they are destined perpetually to increase. As ages roll on they will perpetually multiply, for the sure word of prophecy affirms, "of the increase of His government there shall be no end."

And while the number of the house of Jacob over whom the Prince is to reign will be very great, so also will be the territorial kingdom. It will not be that small portion of land extending from the shores of the Mediterranean sea to a little beyond the river Jordan, and from the southernmost point of the Dead sea to a little north of the lake of Genezareth, including a territory of about nine thousand square miles, which the tribes occupied after their return from Egypt. It is a far greater territory than that, and is truly, in the emphatic language of Scripture, "a good and a large" land, including many other kingdoms or countries beyond the territory occupied by Israel in the days of Joshua and David, and its boundaries are clearly and distinctly marked out in Scripture. In the covenant with Abraham, the Lord defined the western and eastern boundaries of that land, when he said, "Unto thy seed have I given this land, from the river of Egypt" (the Nile) "unto the great river, the river Euphrates." This points out the width of the land, concerning which the greatest mistakes have been made. Instead of extending from the Mediterranean sea to a little beyond the river Jordan, it extends from the Nile over many other kingdoms and countries, till it reaches the far remote Persian gulf and the river Euphrates, which pours its flood of waters gathered from the vast regions of Armenia, Assyria, Mesopotamia, and Shinar into it.

Ezekiel thus points out the boundaries of the land (chap. xlvii. 13–23): "Thus saith the Lord God, This shall be the border whereby ye shall inherit the land, according to the twelve tribes of Israel: Joseph shall have two portions; and ye shall inherit it, one as well as another; concerning the which I lifted up mine hand to give it unto your fathers. And this land shall fall unto you for inheritance. And this shall be the border of the land toward the north side, from the great sea, the way of Hethlon, as men go to Zedab; Hamath, Berothah, Sebraim, which is between the border of Damascus and the border of Hamath; Hazar-hatticon, which is by the coast of Hauran. And the border from the sea shall be Hazar-enan, the border of Damascus, and the north northward, and the border of Hamath. And this is the north side. And the east side ye shall measure from Hauran, and from Damascus, and from Gilead, and from the land of Israel by Jordan, from the border unto the east sea (Persian gulf). And this is the east side...... So shall ye divide this land unto you, according unto the tribes of Israel." Or, in other words, the land of promise, or the land of Israel, is bounded on the west by the great or Mediterranean sea; on the north by the great and extensive range of the mountains of Amanus, running directly to the Euphrates; on the east by the great river Euphrates, flowing into the Persian gulf; and on the south by the Arabian desert; starting from the north side of Kazma bay, in the Persian gulf, running across the great desert, crossing the gulf of Suez, striking the Nile, or as it is called in Scripture, "the great river of Egypt," about twenty miles above the city of Cairo, and a little below Atfieh, then running down the Nile to the Mediterranean sea.

Now that, as clearly pointed out by God himself, is the extent of territory to be possessed by Israel when the covenant with Abraham is fulfilled, and when the Son of the Highest, seated upon the throne of his father David, shall reign over the house of Jacob. It is verily a "large land;" and this we might have expected it would be from the covenant, and the declarations of God concerning it, from the people who were to inhabit it, and from the fact of it being "Immanuel's land." On the north from the Mediterranean sea to the river Euphrates is one hundred miles; on the south from the Nile to the Persian gulf eleven hundred miles; and from north to south five hundred miles; making an area of three hundred thousand square miles. This is a territory greater than any kingdom or empire in Europe, Russia alone excepted. It contains more square miles than the combined territory of the ten kingdoms of Europe, Prussia, Belgium, the Netherlands, Bavaria, Saxony, Hanover, Wurtemburg, Denmark, Sardinia, and Greece. Or it is as large as all the eastern, middle, and half the southern states of our country. Or it is only one third smaller than all our western states. Comparisons like these give us some idea of the vast extent of the land of Israel; and when we look at it by such comparisons, we cannot fail to see the truth of the Bible statement—it is "a large land."

"The Lord formed Israel for his glory, and chose them as his peculiar people; and peculiar too is the land which he assigned them, even as respects its *borders*. The Mediterranean, the Red sea, and the Persian gulf form on the west, the south, and the east borders of a land which, but for these *inland* seas, would be wholly encircled by Asia, Africa, and Europe, and shut out from all direct communication with the Pacific and Atlantic, and the lesser oceans of the globe. The river of Egypt to the Mediterranean, and that sea from the mouth of the Nile to the estuary of the Orontes, and the Euphrates from the foot of Amanus to the Persian gulf, leave not the smallest portion of the west side or of the east side that is not actually or virtually a navigable coast, to the extent on both sides of two thousand miles; while on the north the intermediate barrier of Amanus, at the breadth of less than one hundred, renders the land a garden inclosed."

From its geographical position, *the land of Israel* seems the very centre of the earth. Perhaps there is no land on the face of the globe so surrounded by seas and navigable rivers, which are doubtless God's divinely-prepared highways, not only to carry his peculiar people, the people of the covenant, thither, when the time of their gathering from all lands comes, but also to carry afterwards the converted nations, when they shall go up to Jerusalem from year to year to worship before the Lord the King. From every land, and the islands of the sea, from the rising sun to the farthest west, these highways of waters make easy access and entrance into that land ; and these, much as they may seem trodden now, in the bustle of commerce, are all waiting for the multitudes of travellers yet destined to throng them, their faces all Zionward, when the enraptured cry from that God-honoured and inhabited city shall meet them.

> "From every land they come;
> To see thy beauty, and to share thy joy."

But this "good and large land," a garden inclosed and peculiarly accessible on every side and at every point, and Israel's peculiar inheritance, is not all that shall be theirs, or under their peculiar government, or subservient to them. The surrounding countries, which of old were full of their enemies, shall be inhabited only by their friends; and they, by God's special authority, shall rule over these nations, and they shall be their willing and delighted servants. Instead of the Pharaohs, or any like them, being kings of Egypt, as in the days of old, the princes of Israel, and they only, shall rule there ; and this will add a tributary territory to their land of one hundred and fifty thousand square miles. The kingdom of Mesopotamia too, stretching from the Euphrates to the Tigris ; and of

Assyria, extending from the Tigris to the mountains of Media ; and from Armenia or the Black sea, south to the Persian gulf; and again from the mountains of Media on to the Caspian sea, shall have no king to rule over them, but the divinely-appointed and anointed of Judah and David's princely line, the princes of Israel. All these and other vast kingdoms or empires shall be entirely under Jewish sway, and yield fealty to them and to Him who shall sit upon Israel's throne. They may have their kings, but the princes of Israel, the plenipotentiaries of him who is the Prince of Peace, and the Father of the everlasting age, shall rule over them. All these lands, as well as the land of Israel, shall be under the sceptre of Immanuel ; and they shall bring their wealth and their treasures to him. Oh, how vast, how magnificent this kingdom ! What a beautiful development of the riches of the goodness and munificence of God ! How glorious and extensive the kingdom to be possessed by his people, according to the ancient covenant, and reigned over by his Son, the raised up seed of David, when he shall sit upon his Father's rebuilt throne, and reign over the fully gathered house of Jacob !

According to this, then, the kingdom of Israel shall not only be large, but the people of Israel shall be chief, supreme among the nations. As they were once supreme by the special favour and mighty exalting power of God, though now rejected, despised, and down-trodden in the dust, so shall they be again ; but their next supremacy shall far surpass their former. There they shall be the highly honoured and greatly blessed nation of the *great King*, whom all the nations of the earth shall honour and serve ; the rulers that shall exercise a divine and righteous authority over all countries ; and the light that shall enlighten all lands. That they shall occupy this high and unrivalled position through the exalting power and ever abiding presence of their Lord the King, is clearly, though not extensively nor minutely, set forth in scripture. It is taught in passages like these : "Therefore thy gates shall be open continually ; they shall not be shut day nor night ; that men may bring unto thee the forces of the Gentiles, and that their kings may be brought. For the nation and kingdom that will not serve thee shall perish ; yea, those nations shall be utterly wasted. The sons also of them that afflicted thee shall come bending unto thee ; and all they that despise thee shall bow themselves down at the soles of thy feet ; and they shall call thee, The city of the Lord, The Zion of the Holy One of Israel" (Is. lx. 11–14). "And their seed shall be known among the Gentiles, and their offspring among the people ; all that see them shall acknowledge them that they are the seed which the Lord hath blessed" (Is. lxi. 9). "At that time will I bring you again, even in the time that I gather you ; for I will make you a name and a praise among all people of the earth, when I turn back your captivity before your eyes, saith the Lord" (Zeph. iii. 20). "And all nations shall call you blessed" (Mal. iii. 12). These passages seem sufficient to establish the doctrine, that when Israel inhabit their own large kingdom they will be supreme among the nations. None will dispute their supremacy; none will muster in battle array their vast and well trained forces to overthrow it. All will acknowledge it, from the rising of the sun to the going down of the same; and all will willingly and joyfully pay homage unto it. If any nation dares be delinquent in such service destruction is its certain doom—"it shall perish."

But large as we have seen the land of Canaan, Messiah's kingdom to be, when in glory he shall reign over the house of Jacob, we have not yet seen its full extent. Ah, no. When the heavens reveal Him at the time of the restitution of all things; when he shall come to be Israel's king, they, converted to him as the Messiah, and ready to receive him as such, will, with one voice, exclaim, "Blessed is he that cometh in the name of the Lord!" The veil of Moses being taken from their hearts, and they seeing clearly that this is the Shiloh promised to the fathers, as a nation, they will repent and believe in him. And being thus converted to the true faith, as Christ did before, so he will do again: send them forth missionaries, to preach the gospel of his kingdom to other nations; for the disciples, the seventy, Paul, and Peter, were only types of what they as a nation shall be. Again he will invest the Jews with his divine commission, and send them forth with greater power and success than went the twelve of old. Salvation was first and specially made known unto the Jews, and salvation is of them, for of them Christ came, and they were the first messengers of salvation to the Gentiles. It was through their labours and preaching that the gospel was carried beyond the territory of Judea, and proclaimed in many heathen lands. And again this high, and holy, and honourable work is awaiting them ; for when Messiah comes he declares, "I will send those that escape" (from the battle of Armageddon) "of them unto the nations, to Tarshish, Pul, and Lud, that draw the bow, to Tubal and Javan, to the isles afar off, that have not heard my fame, neither have seen my glory ; and they shall declare my glory among the Gentiles."

That the Jews in this case are to be the messengers sent admits not of a doubt, for they are the persons who will then have specially heard of Messiah's fame and seen his glory ; they are the persons here spoken of as exalted to high posts of special honour ; and while they are to be priests and Levites to the Lord, so also are they to be his messengers to the Gentiles ; to those islands and their inhabitants, and perhaps to others like them, who have not heard his fame nor seen his glory. According to this, another deputation of Jewish missionaries, receiving their commission directly from the Lord the King, as did the apostles of old, shall visit heathen nations, declaring the true character of Messiah ; not merely setting forth his humiliation, suffering, and death, and declaring these to be an atonement for the sins of men, but also proclaiming his resurrection from the dead, and exaltation to boundless, inconceivable glory ; not only revealing him as the crucified, but also as the supremely glorified ; and, by a power peculiarly their own under this new dispensation of missions, proclaiming him the Saviour. This proclamation and glorious preaching, full of such glad tidings, accompanied by the special and all successful blessing and power of him who commissioned them, every Gentile ear will be open to hear, and every heart ready to believe ; to believe in him whom they declare to be the SAVIOUR and the KING, and exalt him to the throne of the affections. No sooner will his name be announced, and his glory declared, than men will believe ; for then Satan's power and influence will have been utterly annihilated, and that of the Lord the King alone will exist in its unopposed mightiness over all the earth ; and then shall the whole of its inhabitants in that great day of his power be a willing people. Satan, the arch deceiver and leader in all earthly revolt, in the bottomless pit, shut up and sealed, will exert no opposing influences ; will not fill the mind with enmity to the truth ; but, under the only and everywhere mighty influence of the only ruling, holy king Jesus, all men will profoundly listen to the glorious proclamation of saving truth ; all will receive the glad tidings, full of great joy, and all will believe. The divinely-commissioned heralds of conversion, the brethren of the great King according to the flesh, running to and fro, shall visit all lands, go into all the earth, preaching these glad tidings, till every ear of man has heard, and every dweller upon the earth believed, in him whom they reveal, until "the earth is full of the knowledge of the Lord, as the waters cover the sea;" until from the rising of the sun even unto the going down of the same, his name shall be great among the Gentiles; and in every place incense shall be offered unto his name, and a pure offering; for his name shall be great among the heathen."

Thus will the reign of peace and blessedness, the glorious millennium, be introduced, and not by missionary operations, as they are carried on in the present day. These may and do serve God's gracious and glorious purposes of gathering a people unto himself from among the Gentiles; a multitude which no man can number, out of every kindred, tongue, and people, and nation; and ought therefore to be carried on with a thousand times more munificent pecuniary contributions, energy, and self-consuming zeal on the part of the Christian church than they have ever been. But great as these efforts may be, involving the whole mightiest energies of the church, they cannot introduce the millennium, because they cannot bind Satan and cast him into the abyss; and while he is at large, as he has been since the seduction of our first parents in Eden, there can be no millennium. Let the missionary of the cross go where he may, sowing the good seed of the word, the wicked one will be there sowing the tares, and under his influence the thorns will spring up and choke the good seed. It will be as it has been for six thousand years. He will keep up in the heart of man hatred of the truth, enmity to God, and rule in the hearts of the children of disobedience. Wherever the sons of God meet to present themselves before the Lord, he will be sure to be among them, exerting his influence to their injury, exciting unhallowed feelings, heartburnings, and divisions. To his evil influences upon the hearts of men, to his mighty opposition to the progress of the truth, there shall be no end while he is at large, like a roaring lion going about seeking whom he may devour. And whatever therefore may be the efforts of the church, and her praiseworthy exertions to convert all nations, yet her mightiest endeavors must ever fail, as they have heretofore done under apostles and the special outpourings of the Holy Spirit, while Satan, the inveterate enemy of the human race, is continually working in the hearts of the children of disobedience. While Satan is at large as he has been, it is manifest from the past there can be no millennium ; and the teachings of scripture are clear and positive on this point, there will be none, until the angel comes down from heaven and binds and shuts up Satan in the bottomless pit, and sets a seal upon him, that he shall deceive the nations no more till the thousand years are fulfilled. The binding and shutting up of Satan, then, is necessary to the introduction and existence of the millennium; and until that is done, no matter what the church does now to Christianize the world, she cannot have the glorious and blessed reign of Christ for which the whole creation is groaning and travailing in pain together.

But when Satan is thus bound and shut up, it is evident that he can no longer exert his deceptive, seductive, soul-destroying influences upon the nations; and his influences being thus utterly removed from the earth, there will be nothing to oppose the truth, or the progress of the truth. Its way being prepared by the great King himself, an universal combination of influences will aid its onward progress. It will appear to every one who hears it to be what it really is, the truth of God, which saves souls, and glorifies its author. It will appear precious, lovely, supremely desirable in its divine beauty, glory, and bliss-giving power. Every heart will intensely desire it, every soul will cordially embrace it. As then the divinely commissioned children of Abraham go forth into this Satan-dispossessed world, and proclaim Christ the Saviour and the King of all nations, as they advance over earth's provinces, men will arise to hail them, as the sleepers of the night arise to welcome the beams of the morning; and receiving the message in faith which they bring, encourage them on their way, on their errand of mercy, in the great work of converting the world. Unbounded prosperity attending their embassy, onward they will go, strong in the might of the Lord, from kingdom to kingdom, from island to island, until they have completed the circuit of the globe—until they have proclaimed the Saviour and his kingdom to the ends of the earth, and all nations, enlightened and Christianized, fall down and worship him, and call him blessed. Thus and then the millennium will be introduced; the stone, cut out of the mountain without hands, become a great mountain, and fill the whole earth; the kingdoms of this world become the kingdoms of our Lord and of his Christ; the dwellers on the earth be all righteous. Then will

> "One song employ all nations; and all cry,
> Worthy the Lamb, for he was slain for us!
> The dwellers in the vales and on the rock
> Shout to each other, and the mountain tops
> From distant mountains catch the flying joy;
> And nation after nation taught the strain,
> Earth roll the rapturous hosanna round."

Then will have been heard and fully answered by God the beautiful prayer of David, the sweet singer of Israel, as recorded in the sixty-seventh psalm, which teaches the conversion of the Jewish nation, and through them and their instrumentality the conversion of the world. For then will "God have been merciful to the Jewish nation, and blessed them, and caused his face to shine upon them; then will his way be known upon the earth, and his saving health among all nations; then shall the nations be glad and sing for joy; then shall he judge the people righteously and govern the nations upon earth. Then shall the people praise Him ; all the people praise Him. Then shall the earth yield her increase, and Israel's God shall bless them. God shall bless them ; and all the ends of the earth shall fear Him." When this glorious consummation, the conversion of the world, by the conversion and instrumentality of converted Israel, has been accomplished, " then there shall be one King and one Lord, and his name one over all the earth." Then shall the Son of the highest sitting universal King upon the rebuilt throne of his father David, reign over and bless the house of Jacob, which is the head of the Israelitish nation, and is here used to denote the whole of that "peculiar people," and through Jacob or his seed, which in number are to be like unto the stars of heaven or the sand upon the sea shore, reign over and bless all the families of the earth. The extent then of the kingdom or territorial domain over which Christ, when He sits upon his promised, his covenanted throne, will be not only the Land of Judea, but the *whole habitable globe*.

Such is the precious and enrapturing truth clearly taught by all the holy men of God, who spake as they were moved by the Holy Ghost, when that kingdom by divine revelation was presented to their view, and they described its surpassing glory and vast extent. They represent it as not merely the land of covenant, the land of Canaan—though that is strictly and peculiarly the kingdom, the land specially to be occupied by

Israel and Israel's Prince; but, they represent the kingdom, as we have already seen, as extending beyond that territory, emphatically designated "Immanuel's land," and comprehending the whole earth; they represent Him as a King with whom no one divides any of earth's territory; but who occupies it all as his own. Satan thoroughly dispossessed, He alone, with his divine holy sceptre, rules over every continent, every island. There is not one spot from pole to pole, from the remote east to the farthest west, but forms a part of His kingdom and is under his immediate government. And hence David said, when speaking of the great dominion or kingdom of his Son, "He shall reign from sea to sea; from the river unto the ends of the earth. All kings shall fall down before him, all nations shall serve him. His name shall endure for ever. His name shall continue as long as the sun; and men shall be blessed in him; *all nations* shall call him blessed. And blessed be his glorious name for ever; and let the *whole earth* be filled with his glory." Isaiah sang, chap. ix. 6, 7, "Unto us a child is born, unto us a son is given; and the government shall be upon his shoulder; and his name shall be called Wonderful, Counsellor, The Mighty God, The Father of the everlasting age, The Prince of Peace. Of the increase of his government and peace there shall be no end, upon the throne of David, and upon his kingdom, to order it, and to establish it with judgment and with justice from henceforth even for ever." Daniel said, "I saw in the night visions, and behold one like the Son of man came with the clouds of heaven, and came to the Ancient of days, and they brought him near before him. And there was given him dominion, and glory, and a kingdom, *that all people, nations, and languages, should serve him!* And the kingdom, and dominion, *and the greatness of the kingdom under the whole heaven* shall be given to the people of the saints of the Most High, whose kingdom is an everlasting kingdom, and all dominions shall serve and obey him." Zachariah said, " And the Lord shall be king *over all the earth;* in that day shall there be one Lord, and his name one." When the seventh apocalyptic angel sounded, John heard great voices in heaven saying, " The kingdoms of this world are become the kingdoms of our Lord and his Christ; and he shall reign for ever and ever."

According, then, to the clear and uniform teaching of the holy Scriptures, the kingdom over which Christ in person is to reign, when he shall sit upon the throne of his father David, and reign over the house of Jacob, is *the whole earth.* He is not merely to reign over the land of Judea, peculiarly His land, destined according to prophecy to be greatly enlarged at the return of the Jews, but over this entire globe. The earth itself and nothing less shall be his kingdom. Satan, who has been so long the prince of the power of the air, and exercised his authority with such despotic sway, shall be dispossessed of his power by Jesus the prince of peace, who shall then be sovereign in the region in which, for nigh six thousand years, he has been planning and working out his purposes of wickedness with such dreadful influence upon the children of men. He who has been so long the God of this world ; and has kept millions of our race in soul-enthralling, soul-destroying bondage to himself, shall be divested of all his honour and influence when the strong angel comes down from heaven, binds him, casts him into the bottomless pit, or abyss, shuts him up and sets a seal upon him. Then shall his kingdom be completely taken from him—not one inch of this earth's surface will belong to him—in not one locality of the earth will his power be acknowledged or obeyed. The place where he has so long reigned, and perpetrated such awful deeds of wickedness and cruelty—seduced and destroyed the souls of men—moved them to crucify the Lord of Glory, and rob the Most High of the honour righteously belonging to him, shall become solely the dominion of the King of Glory, and the Government being exclusively upon his shoulder, his sceptre of righteousness and peace shall be swayed over the whole of this earth, redeemed from vanity and the curse. "He shall reign from sea to sea, from the river unto the ends of the earth." The groaning and painful travail of the whole creation shall cease; and instead of the wail of agony, long, loud, and piercing, which has everywhere gone up in unutterable sorrow, shall ascend the song of unmingled joy—of heartfelt peace and blessedness, to him who sitteth as rightful Lord upon the throne of his own redeemed creation.

For thus saith he, who shall have the crown upon his head and the sceptre in his hand, "from the rising of the sun, even unto the going down of the same, my name shall be great among the Gentiles ; and in every place incense shall be offered unto my name, and a pure offering." Mal. i. 11.

And let it not be forgotten that this vast kingdom of peace, righteousness, and blessedness, including the whole earth, over which the Son of the Highest, seated upon the throne of his father David is to reign, is a literal kingdom, a kingdom, as we have seen, upon earth renewed. The literality and universality of it are both clearly set forth in Daniel. The monarchies symbolized by Nebuchadnezzar's great image, the Chaldean, the Persian, the Grecian, and Roman, were literal monarchies, and had a literal existence upon the earth, and clearly defined boundaries. The Medo-Persian vanquished the Babylonian, the Grecian vanquished the Medo-Persian, and the Roman vanquished the Grecian. The Roman Empire is now existing in its divided state —in the ten kingdoms symbolized by the ten toes, and trembling before the onward progress of the mighty overturning movements, which under the guiding hand of God will crush them to the dust, overthrow their thrones, and scatter their sceptres as worthless things. Now as all these were literal kingdoms, including a certain territory or definite portion of the earth, so also must the fifth monarchy, or Christ's kingdom, almost everywhere spoken against, be a literal kingdom including, as we have seen, a certain extent. And this is most clearly taught by Daniel, both in his description and explanation of Nebuchadnezzar's great image. "The stone cut out of the mountain without hands," symbolizes the fifth monarchy or kingdom, which is Christ's, which "the God of heaven will set up," evidently upon the earth, utterly destroys the remnants of its power, and takes possession of that very territory for itself. For the stone that smites the image, or rather the toes of the image, becomes a great mountain, and fills not only the territory of these monarchies, but rolls on in its irresistible growing greatness, till it fills *the whole earth*—takes possession of the habitable globe, extending from sea to sea, "from the river unto the ends of the earth." Over this divine kingdom peculiarly, emphatically the Lord's, embracing all kingdoms under the whole heavens—*the earth itself* Messiah's kingdom, the cry shall be heard from every place uttered by every tongue, "The Lord God omnipotent reigneth."

"Zion's King shall reign victorious,
All the earth shall own his sway;
He will make the kingdom glorious,
He shall reign through endless day.

"Nations, now from God estranged,
Then shall see a glorious light;
Night to day shall then be changed,
Heaven shall triumph in the sight.

"See the ancient idols falling,
Worshipped once but now abhorred,
Men on Zion's King are calling,
Zion's King by all adored.

"Then shall Israel long dispersed,
Mourning seek their Lord and God.
Look on him whom once they pierced,
Own and kiss the chastening rod.

"Then shall Israel all be saved,
War and tumult then shall cease,
While the greater Son of David
Rules a conquered world in peace."

Such, then, according to the sure word of prophecy is the extent of the kingdom which shall be given unto Jesus, when the Son of the Highest shall sit upon the throne of his father David; such shall constitute the kingdom of God upon earth—the millennial blessedness—the glory of the latter days. Was there ever a kingdom like this, knowing no bounds but the habitable globe; knowing no king but the Lord Jesus Christ; having no throne but the rebuilt throne of David; no government but the pure and holy authority of Immanuel; submitting to no sceptre but his—his will being done on earth as in heaven! "The kingdoms of this world have become the kingdoms of our Lord and of his Christ." "Glory dwells in the land. Mercy and truth have met together; righteousness and peace kiss each other. Truth springs out of the earth renewed, and righteousness looks down from heaven. Yea, the Lord gives that which is good, and the land yields her increase." "All people fall down before him, and all nations call him blessed."

> "Haste then, and wheel away a shattered world,
> Ye slow revolving seasons! we would see
> (A sight to which our eyes are strangers yet)
> A world that does not dread and hate his laws,
> And suffer for its crime; would learn how fair
> The creature is that God pronounces good,
> And pleasant in itself what pleases Him."

What kingdom in glory and blessedness is once to be compared to this kingdom—the kingdom of the LORD JESUS CHRIST? It stands without a rival, without a compeer; alone—matchless in glory and blessedness. The king is there, and his presence is felt throughout its vast domains, inspiring all with a holy, boundless joy. His children are there; his redeemed ones—all purified from the pollution of sin; all arrayed in linen clean and white, the righteousness of saints—all radiant as the sun—all rapturous in joy. Who longs not to inherit this kingdom? What heart burns not with most intense desire to be the heir of this kingdom? Surely not yours, reader! If you can realize the glory and blessedness of this kingdom, like the thief on the cross when his eyes were opened to the divine scene, there will be but one all-absorbing desire in your bosom, and that will be for Christ to remember you, and take you into this kingdom at His coming. For that you will pray without ceasing; for that you will renounce the world; for that you will crucify the flesh with its affections and lusts; for that you will be willing to forsake all the dear and beloved ones on earth; for that you will be willing to lay down your life. Any thing and every thing to attain this kingdom—to be an heir of this kingdom, "the inheritance of Christ and of the saints in light." Ah! yes; to attain this the most precious inheritance, the most glorious and blessed of all habitations, you will ever be examining your own heart to see if there is any good evidence of obtaining the kingdom. You will be scrutinizing your affections to see if they are really set upon the kingdom of Messiah; and you will not rest till you have the satisfactory evidence of God's Spirit within you, that with Christ Jesus you are an heir of all things, and consequently an heir of his kingdom.

If you are a believer in Jesus, then you can be looking forward to the inheritance of that kingdom with the most rapturous emotions and thrilling joy, for that kingdom is yours by covenant and promise, and will soon be yours by actual possession. You will soon move among its shining inhabitants, glorious as they; you will soon be a participant of its supreme and everlasting blessedness. The short-lived sorrows of time need not distress you here; like the morning cloud these will soon pass away, and be succeeded by "the exceeding and eternal weight of glory," and joy in the kingdom. Sink not under the griefs of the present night of weeping, for through its darkest gloom and deepest distress some comforting beams of the cloudless joy-light of the coming Kingdom are struggling; and endless joy cometh in the morning of the eternal day—the morning of the ushering in of the kingdom. There remaineth a rest for the people of God and that rest will be yours. "With Abraham, Isaac, and Jacob you shall sit down in the kingdom."

But if you are not a believer in Christ—what then? Solemn, awful thought; you cannot be admitted into the kingdom. Ah! no, you cannot. You must and will be excluded unless you believe. Christ is inviting you by his word, urging you by his obedience, suffering, and death to believe in him, and enter into his kingdom of matchless, boundless glory and blessedness. If you believe you shall be admitted; if you remain in unbelief, true indeed a kingdom shall be yours; but it will be the kingdom of misery, and darkness, and eternal death. You may not now realize what will be the awfulness of your situation then; and when you actually feel it, it will be too late to change it. Are you willing to be consigned to the kingdom of eternal misery, darkness, and death? Surely you cannot be! Your soul must shudder at such a thought, and shrink with unutterable horror from such a doom. If this be so, then hasten to Jesus the almighty Saviour —believe in him that you may be saved, and welcomed with the multitude of redeemed into "the kingdom of God and his dear Son."

CHAPTER III.

THE DURATION OF MESSIAH'S KINGDOM.

"He shall reign over the house of Jacob *for ever;* And of his kingdom there shall be no end."—LUKE i. 33.

WE have seen by the clear light of prophecy, that Jesus Christ is to sit upon the throne of his father David. That throne once occupied by David in Jerusalem, which for thousands of years has been, and still is in ruins, is destined by God's unchangeable oracle to be rebuilt and occupied by the raised up humanity of the Son of the virgin—by the Man-God, Christ Jesus. That throne is to be erected upon earth, and occupied by the Lord the King for ever. "The Lord God *shall* give unto him the throne of his father David." As David literally occupied a throne upon the earth, so shall the Son of the virgin, the Son of the Highest, literally occupy that throne rebuilt; for the sure word of prophecy repeatedly declares, he shall sit upon the throne of his father David.

When He ascends that throne, he is to reign over the house of Jacob. The house of Jacob, we have seen, is used to denote all the believing descendants of Jacob—of Abraham, and that when Christ returns to earth to occupy that throne, all the believing seed of Abraham slumbering in their graves shall be raised, and all his living seed shall be converted and brought from the four winds of heaven into their own land, the land of Israel, which is the land of covenant and promise. Exalted to the throne of his own peculiar kingdom, and reigning over that, his own land, his brethren according to the flesh converted, and re-baptized with more than a double portion of the missionary spirit—Satan, the great author of evil and adversary of men, cast into the bottomless pit, they go forth everywhere, preaching the gospel, and all who hear believe, till all nations are converted, and "the kingdoms of this world become the kingdoms of our Lord and of his Christ."

Having seen Messiah exalted to his royal throne, and reigning over "the kingdoms and the greatness of the kingdoms under the whole heavens," we come now to consider the duration of that reign upon the earth, which the angel Gabriel describes in these words to his mother, "He shall reign over the house of Jacob *for ever;* and of his kingdom there shall be no end." If we rightly understand the teachings of scripture that reign upon and over the earth will be *eternal.* Be not surprised at this announcement, but hear patiently and candidly the teachings of scripture, and if they furnish not conclusive evidence, that Christ seated upon the throne of his father David, shall reign over the house of Jacob for ever, upon this earth renewed, it is your duty to reject such a doctrine; but if they *do teach*, that in person he shall reign for ever upon this earth, then by heaven's authority you are bound to believe it. And the moment you see it with heavenly unscaled eyes you will believe, and you will rejoice in believing it, with an ecstacy of joy such as has never thrilled through your bosom.

The earth renewed, we say, is to be the place or scene of Christ's eternal reign with his redeemed and glorified people. In order to prove this doctrine, it is manifestly necessary at the very outset, to prove that the earth must exist for ever. And the evidence to prove the everlasting duration of the earth must be deduced from the word of God; and some of its teachings upon this subject shall now be examined.

In Psalm xciii. 1, it is thus written, "The Lord reigneth, he is clothed with majesty; the Lord is clothed with strength, wherewith he hath girded himself: the world also is established that it cannot be moved," or rather as it is in the original, "yea, he hath established the world that it *shall* not be moved." If according to this language the world is established that it cannot, or *shall* not be moved, then beyond all controversy, it is destined to endure for ever; its eternal existence is secured. If it shall not be moved it must remain, and remaining, continue to remain; and hence its everlasting duration is declared in the strongest language. If this is not what this psalm teaches, it is difficult to know what it does teach. It represents the Lord Jehovah as the king reigning over this earth, and to show that his reign and kingdom shall never have an end, it is declared that the world shall not be moved. But if the world is destroyed, if it is annihilated, then it is moved, it is more than moved ; it ceases to exist, and the solemn declaration of this psalm is falsified ; the Lord doth not reign over it, neither is he clothed with Jehovah strength for its glorious government.

The eternal duration of the earth is also clearly and positively taught in Psalm civ. 5 : " The Lord laid the foundations of the earth, that it should not be removed for ever," or as it might have been rendered, " He hath founded the earth upon its settlements, that it should not be moved for ever, even for ever." Ponder that declaration ; for surely if language can express eternal duration, this language expresses it, this describes it, and consequently declares the eternal duration of the earth. If it shall not be moved for ever, even for ever, then it evidently abides and that for ever. There is no destruction, no reduction to nonentity awaiting it. There is, there can be no other conclusion. To deny this, would be to deny one of the plainest and strongest declarations of holy writ ; and to attempt to explain it away, would be like endeavouring to prove that it is midnight darkness, when the blazing beams of the meridian sun are blinding the eyes with their excessive brightness. It will not do to say, that all that this language means, simply is, that it is established till the end of its creation be fulfilled: that is, till a definite number of generations of mankind have existed as they now exist. The language implies no condition of this kind. It is absolute. Neither can any man prove, that at any given point of the progression of our race the earth will have fulfilled the end of its creation. On the contrary, we contend that it never will have fulfilled the end of its creation—that it will be no longer useful, and therefore shall cease to exist; for God positively and solemnly declares, he will use it for ever, as we shall see more fully by and by.

The same doctrine is taught with equal perspicuity and force by the wise man, Ecc. i. 4, when he says, "One generation passeth away and another generation cometh, but the earth *abideth for ever.*" Here a succession of generations is declared. No generation abides: one goes and another comes, only to go in like manner. Transition, end, are declared concerning each one of them; but it is not so with the earth; it passeth not away: it has no end; it abides for ever. And its ever enduring existence is one of the grand truths, if not *the* grand truth taught in the passage. The passing generations of men, and the ever abiding earth are placed in striking contrast; and this is done by the infinite wisdom of God, not so much to impress us with the transitoriness of the generations of men, as the ever abiding, the eternal duration of the earth.

The perpetuity of the earth is also taught by Paul in

Heb. i. 10–12, "And thou, Lord, in the beginning hast laid the foundation of the earth; and the heavens are the works of thine hands: they shall perish, but thou remainest; and they all shall wax old as doth a garment: and as a vesture shalt thou fold them up, and they shall be changed; but thou art the same, and thy years shall not fail." Some may suppose that in this passage, they see the destruction, the annihilation of the heavens and the earth clearly taught, when it is here said they shall perish. But the word here rendered perish, does not mean destruction or annihilation, in any instance where it occurs in the New Testament, but to send away, to release, to set at liberty, to dismiss. It occurs about seventy times, and has in every instance some of these shades of meaning, and might have been almost uniformly translated, release, and might with propriety have been so translated in this passage; "They shall be released." This would be in perfect accordance with the passage, for the Apostle does not affirm that they shall perish or be destroyed; but that they shall be changed. The word rendered changed, does not mean annihilated, but changed, altered, or transformed. If by perish he had meant that they shall be annihilated, he would certainly not have been so self-contradictory as to say in the same sentence they shall be changed, altered, or transformed. The change shall not be, as is evident from this and many passages of Scripture, unto perdition, or utter destruction, but to perfect restitution. They shall be loosed, or released from the effects of sin—from the curse, and changed or transformed to perfect holiness : and then, in this changed, transformed, renewed, or restituted condition, according to the immutable teachings of God's word, they shall abide or endure for ever. And this change is produced that the earth, destined to exist for ever, may exist in perfection and glory. And Paul, in the preceding verses of this chapter, clearly teaches in his quotations, that this changed or renewed earth shall be the locality of the Son's throne which is for ever and ever ; and the kingdom over which his sceptre of righteousness shall be eternally swayed, and this unquestionably implies and teaches the eternal existence of the earth.

The teaching of Peter in his second epistle, chap. iii. 10–13, proves the same doctrine ; "But the day of the Lord will come as a thief in the night ; in the which the heavens shall pass away with a great noise, and the elements shall melt with fervent heat, the earth also, and the works that are therein, shall be burnt up. Seeing then, that all these things shall be dissolved, what manner of persons ought we to be in all holy conversation and godliness : looking for, and hastening unto the coming of the day of God, wherein the heavens, being on fire, shall be dissolved, and the elements shall melt with fervent heat, nevertheless we, according to his promise, look for new heavens and a new earth, wherein dwelleth righteousness."

Though this passage may seemingly teach the destruction or annihilation of the earth, yet it does not in verity teach this gloomy doctrine, but the very reverse. The expression "burnt up," has led some to suppose and believe, that this earth will be utterly consumed, destroyed, or annihilated by fire or burning. The language here used, "burnt up," seems to involve such an idea. It seems to imply utterly consumed, but the Greek word does not convey this idea. It is compounded of the verb καιω to burn, and the preposition κατα, which signifies down, down upon, from above. The literal translation then of this word is not "burnt up" but burnt down upon, burnt from above. The passage would then read thus, "the earth and the works that are therein shall be burnt from above." That is to say, the fire will be kindled upon the earth from above. The atmosphere, after God Almighty has produced certain changes upon it, which it is not necessary here to explain, will be set on fire first, and the burning atmosphere will set fire to the earth and the works that are thereon. As the atmosphere is everywhere above the earth, and as that has to set fire to the earth, the earth will be burnt down upon, or burnt from above.

This then contains nothing of the idea of burning to destruction, of burning to annihilation. It teaches the doctrine that the earth shall be subjected to the action of fire, but it also teaches that the result of that action will not be the utter consuming of this earth from among the works of God; its utter extinction from the things which declare his eternal power and Godhead. This

Peter proves by unanswerable argument. When the Old world was overflowed with water and perished, the earth was not reduced to nonentity—the earth continued to exist. If then the water did not annihilate the earth, and we know and are witnesses this day it did not, for it sprang in undiminished materiality from the assuaging waters; neither will the fire or burning which awaits it. This is Peter's very argument. As the earth survived the action of the water, so will it survive the action of the fire; and consequently despite of this burning, which will produce great, and important, and glorious changes upon it, he says, "nevertheless we, according to his promise," that is the promise of God uttered by Isaiah, "look for a new heaven and a new earth, wherein dwelleth righteousness."

This then settles the point, that the earth shall not be burnt up—shall not, like "the baseless fabric of a vision pass away," shall not be annihilated, or cease to exist among the works of God. After the burning it shall continue to occupy its place. It shall retain its form and local identity. Sinai, and Olivet, and Calvary, and Zion, where the great king is to sit and reign in glory; and Jordan too, in whose refreshing waters Messiah, in the days of his humiliation, often bathed his weary feet; and the river of Egypt, and the great river, the river Euphrates, will all remain after the conflagration, and be better known and more frequently visited than they are now. The burning of the heavens, or atmosphere, and the earth, is not then a burning unto destruction, but a burning unto purification. And when these have been thus purified, then out of these so purified elements will come the new heavens and the new earth. As the earth of old emerged in renovated freshness from the subsiding of the deluge, so the new heavens and the new earth, all purified, all perfect, all glorious, all smiling and sparkling in the holiness of their great Redeemer, will emerge, amidst the shouts of angels, the songs of the morning stars, the hallelujahs of the redeemed, from the subsiding or expiring flames of the conflagration.

And if this earth is once made new, and made new, too, for the dwelling-place of righteousness; that is for God's righteous people made righteous by the imputation of Christ's righteousness, and for Jehovah their righteousness, as the apostle manifestly asserts; then surely there can be no motive, no reason for its destruction or annihilation; but its own perfection and holiness; and it being the dwelling-place of the Lord's holy and righteous people, and of the Lord our righteousness himself, are all sufficient reasons to save it from destruction, and prolong its existence for ever and ever.

Now it is manifest that these passages do not teach the utter destruction or annihilation of the earth; but only that it is destined to be the subject of certain great and important changes. These changes, instead of deteriorating it, will result in the great and glorious improvement for which the whole creation is now groaning and travailing in pain together. They will purify it from the effects of sin, and restore it to a condition in which it will again be very good in the sight of God, and fitted to endure eternally in its goodness before him. And if these passages do not teach the utter destruction of the earth, its annihilation from among the vast and glorious works of God, but on the contrary its perpetuity, its everlasting existence ; then it may be safely contended that there is not one passage in the Bible that teaches or even hints the gloomy doctrine, that this earth shall be finally destroyed ; that it shall be burnt up, and its very ashes consumed, so that nothing of it shall remain.

But the Bible abounds with passages teaching directly and indirectly the *eternal* existence of the earth. They pervade it from beginning to end. Were they carefully collected they would form a vast number, and time would fail to examine minutely such a great cloud of witnesses and closely scrutinize their testimony, which would be found various in kind, yet perfectly in unison as regards the grand point to be established—all testifying with united voice, "the earth which God has given to the sons of men and his own Son as their king, yet destined to rejoice with him in its habitable parts *shall endure for ever and ever*." Satisfied with this brief proof of the earth's eternal existence, we shall next consider, shortly, what evidence there is of Christ reigning eternally with his glorified saints upon this ever enduring earth.

The personal return of Christ to earth is a doctrine clearly and certainly taught, and very frequently referred to in Scripture. Enoch the seventh from Adam taught this doctrine in his beautiful evangelical sermon preached to the early inhabitants of the earth. "Behold the Lord cometh with ten thousand of his saints to execute judgment upon all, and to convince all that are ungodly among them of all their ungodly deeds, which they have ungodly committed, and of all their hard speeches which ungodly sinners have spoken against them." Moses, and all the prophets, and David in the psalms are ever and anon teaching the glorious doctrine of the Lord's second advent, and with ineffable delight expatiating upon it. Of this the whole of the ninety-sixth psalm is a beautiful example, though we quote only the three concluding verses. "Let the heavens rejoice, and let the earth be glad; let the sea roar, and the fulness thereof. Let the field be joyful, and all that is therein; then shall all the trees of the wood rejoice before the Lord; for he cometh, for he cometh to judge the earth: he shall judge the world with righteousness, and the people with his truth." The Lord himself is continually teaching, and referring to his personal return to earth—ever reminding his disciples that they "shall see the Son of man coming in the clouds of heaven with power and great glory." The apostle makes very frequent mention of the same event, and holds up in some way or other to the minds of the individuals whom they addressed "that blessed hope, and the glorious appearing of the great God and our Saviour Jesus Christ." And this doctrine is so held up because of its great, precious, comforting, and sanctifying influence.

And if Christ's return to earth is so frequently and clearly taught, it is fearlessly contended, that after he has come it is nowhere taught that he will leave this earth. That passage so frequently referred to, by no means makes out the point or even touches it. 1 Thess. iv. 17 : "Then we which are alive and remain shall be caught up together with them in the clouds, to meet the Lord in the air : and so shall we ever be with the Lord." Caught up, for what purpose? To meet the Lord. And what then? Accompany him back to paradise whence he came, or some other orb in creation? No. He is on his way to earth to judgment and they are caught up to meet him, not that they may depart from the earth, but that they may accompany him to this earth, and to the great work of judgment before him. This, too, takes place before the judgment, and consequently does not prove that Christ and his people shall leave this earth after the judgment, but that the saints shall be caught up to meet him coming to the judgment, and upon meeting him shall return and accompany him to earth and judgment. The would-be-eloquent pulpit rhetorical flourishes then of his leaving this earth with all his saints after the judgment, and carrying them with him, no man knows whither, are not based upon the teachings of God's word, but originate in the erring imaginations of man. When he comes to earth he comes as judge: he comes as its restitutor—as its creator anew—he comes as its ever-abiding and reigning king.

That Christ will reign for ever upon the earth is clearly implied, if not distinctly taught in the covenant made with Abraham. In that covenant God said to Abraham, Isaac, and Jacob, "to thee and to thy seed will I give this land for an everlasting possession." Now if Abraham and his seed are to inherit that land for ever, as the covenant most clearly declares—if they are to be brought up out of their graves, and from all countries, whither God in his anger has driven them, as the Holy Ghost teaches, that they may dwell in their own land, the land of Israel for ever; then must Christ their king reign over them in the earth for ever. "He shall reign over the house of Jacob for ever, and of his kingdom there shall be no end."

The perpetuity of Messiah's kingdom and personal reign upon the earth, are as clearly and positively taught as language can teach them. David sang, Ps. lxxii. 17, "His name shall endure for ever: his name shall be continued as long as the sun; and all men shall be blessed in him; all nations shall call him blessed." It is admitted by all that this psalm is descriptive of Messiah's glorious reign and kingdom upon earth, and if so then these words assert their perpetuity—"His name shall endure for ever." This language is expressive of interminable duration; and if his name has to endure for ever, then so long has he to reign upon the earth; for the duration of his name is spoken of in connexion with his reign; and consequently his reign must be coeval with the duration of his name. His name here is synonymous with his reign; and when it is said his name shall endure for ever, it means that his reign and kingdom shall endure for ever. During the continuance of his name and his coëval reign, all men are to be blessed in him, and during that endless reign all the nations of the earth are to call Him blessed. But if the reign here spoken of be not eternal then the blessings to be bestowed upon the nations of the earth through it, will not by them be eternally enjoyed. When the reign terminates, the blessings, of course, which it bestows will also terminate; and after enjoying these for so long they will ultimately be deprived of them. But during this reign, too, the nations of the earth are to call Messiah blessed, and if it come to an end so will these ascriptions of praise to Him from the nations come to an end. But God has provided against such gloomy results as these, and for eternal blessings from the great king during his endless reign to his people, and for their ceaseless ascriptions of praise in return to Him; for he said, "I will make thy name to be remembered in all generations; therefore shall the people praise thee for ever and ever."

Ps. xcvi. 10: "Say among the heathen," or Gentiles, "the Lord reigneth; the world also shall be established, that it cannot be moved; he shall judge the people righteously." This forms a part of another of these triumphal odes, celebrating Christ's kingly rule upon the earth, and teaching clearly the everlasting duration of that reign. When it is once introduced it will be perpetual, for the earth is established for ever that it may be perpetual; and that during that endless reign he may judge the people righteously. "Thy throne, O God, is *for ever and ever;* the sceptre of thy kingdom is a right sceptre." "My mercy will I keep for him *for ever more*, and my covenant shall stand fast with him. His seed also will I make to *endure for ever*, and his throne as the days of heaven." "Once have I sworn by my holiness, that I will not lie unto David," or the Beloved. "His seed shall *endure for ever*, and his throne *as the sun before me*." "Thy kingdom is an *everlasting* kingdom; and thy dominion *endureth throughout all generations*." "The Lord shall reign *for ever*, even thy God, O Zion, unto all generations."

Surely language could not be constructed more clearly expressing perpetuity—eternal duration, than that of the passages just quoted. But these passages describe the duration of Christ's reign and government upon earth; consequently that reign and government must be eternal. And it is beyond all controversy their very object to teach this doctrine. It is vain to attempt to limit the meaning of these passages by saying that they only express a long period of time, and when this earth comes to an end so will that reign; for we have already proved that the earth, after having undergone certain changes, will endure for ever.

Isaiah clearly teaches the perpetuity of Messiah's reign in these words, chap. ix. 6, 7: "For unto us a child is born, unto us a Son is given; and the government shall be upon his shoulder; and his name shall be called Wonderful, Counsellor, the mighty God, the everlasting Father," or the Father of the everlasting age, "the Prince of Peace. *Of the increase of his government and peace there shall be no end,* upon the throne of David and upon his kingdom, to order it, and *to establish* it with judgment and with justice from *henceforth even for ever.* The zeal of the Lord of Hosts will perform this." In this passage Jesus Christ, the Messiah is called the Father of the everlasting age, for so the clause ought to be rendered. And the age here spoken of, in the very nature of things, must be future, the age of His government when he introduces His kingdom, and sits down upon the throne of His father David. That age of kingly government and rule, which he will then introduce, and of which he will be the father, is declared to be *everlasting.* And to exclude the very possibility of doubt on this very important point, it is affirmed, that of the increase of His government and peace there shall be no end, and if of them no end, then surely they shall last for ever. Nor is this all, but to make it yet more certain that His reign shall be upon the earth and eternal, it is added, "upon," that is, He shall sit and reign "upon the throne of his father David and upon His kingdom to order it, and to establish it with judgment and with justice from henceforth *even for ever.*"

"Behold the days come, saith the Lord, that I will perform that good thing which I promised to the house of Israel, and to the house of Judah. In those days and at that time, will I cause the Branch of righteousness to grow up unto David; and he shall execute judgment and righteousness in the land. In those days shall Judah be saved, and Jerusalem shall dwell safely; and this is the name whereby he shall be called, The Lord our Righteousness. For thus saith the LORD, *David shall never want a man to sit* upon the throne of the house of Israel." Jer. xxxiii. 11–18: "Say unto them, thus saith the LORD GOD, Behold, I will take the children of Israel from among the heathen, whither they be gone, and will gather them on every side, and bring them into their own land; and I will make them one nation in the land upon the mountain of Israel; and one KING shall be king to them all; and they shall be no more two nations, neither shall they be divided into two kingdoms any more at all; neither shall they defile themselves any more with their idols, nor with their detestable things, nor with any of their transgressions; but I will save them out of all their dwelling-places, wherein they have sinned, and will cleanse them; so shall they be my people, and I will be their GOD. And DAVID," or the BELOVED, "my servant shall be king over them all; and they all shall have one shepherd ; they shall also walk in my judgments and observe my statutes, and do them. And they shall dwell in the land that I have given unto Jacob my servant, wherein your fathers have dwelt ; and they shall dwell therein, even they, and their children, and their children's children *for ever ;* and my servant David, or BELOVED, shall be their prince *for ever.* Moreover, I will make a covenant of peace with them ; it shall be an everlasting covenant with them ; and I will place them and multiply them, and will set my sanctuary in the midst of them for *evermore.*" "My tabernacle also shall be with them ; yea I will be their God and they shall be my people. And the heathen, Gentiles, shall know that I the Lord do sanctify Israel, when my sanctuary shall be in the midst of them for *evermore.*" Ezek. xxxvii. 21–28.

Daniel contemplating the same glorious and enrapturing scene said, chap. i. 44, "And in the days of these kings ; that is in the days of the last kings ;" or at the close of the remnant of the Roman dynasty, "shall the God of heaven set up a kingdom which *shall never be destroyed ;* and the kingdom shall not be left to other people, but it shall break in pieces and consume all these kingdoms, *and shall stand for ever.*"

The kingdom which the God of heaven shall set up in the days of the last kings of the Roman dynasties or ten kingdoms, is doubtless Messiah's kingdom ; for it cannot be supposed that the God of heaven would set up any other. Besides, the description of the kingdom perfectly accords with that everywhere given of Messiah's kingdom. It is to the destruction of the ten kingdoms he is to come, and at that time introduce and set up Messiah's kingdom; and that kingdom is here declared to be a kingdom that *shall never be destroyed.* And if it is never to be destroyed, surely in its utter exemption, or divine protection from destruction, it must and will exist for ever. If this is not the meaning of Daniel's language, it may well be asked what does it mean? Does it mean not eternal but limited duration? If it does, how then or by what language shall we express endless duration?

But the kingdom of Messiah to be set up at that time, is not only a kingdom never to be destroyed but a kingdom that shall break in pieces, consume, or destroy all these kingdoms, and not only these but all others upon the face of the earth. No kingdom is to coexist with it. It is to stand alone and be universal. It is to be introduced by destroying others, and that work of destruction it will begin upon the ten Roman kingdoms. And as it is altogether divine and holy in its nature, and essentially different from any existing upon the face of the earth, it will continue to consume the existing kingdoms until they are all destroyed. In its consuming progress it will continue to extend until it sweeps away every vestige of the previous kingdoms, and appears in its all-pervading greatness, and takes possession of the whole earth from the rising of the sun to the going down of the same. And when it has done all this, when it becomes in reality, the *one kingdom*, claiming for its dominion the whole earth, and swaying its sceptre over every individual that dwells thereon, the prophet declares "it shall *stand for ever.*" This declaration again teaches its eternal duration, and this truth the prophet reiterates, that it may be observed, that it may be believed. It appears that he was under the apprehension that men would doubt the doctrine, and hence he again and again asserts it. The kingdom of Messiah then, once established upon the earth, and existing alone in its divine power and perfection, there will be no kingdom to assail it in ruinous hostilities, no puissant arm to overthrow its immovable throne, and no mighty foot to tread in the dust, the glorious crown destined to flourish for ever upon its Sovereign's head. That kingdom existing upon a divinely redeemed and renewed earth, incorruptible, undefiled and that cannot fade away, shall, so far as the place of its existence is concerned, be prolonged through endless ages. The omniscient and omnipotent God-Man being at its head, its affairs will be managed with infinite wisdom, and sustained by almighty power, and prolonged through "the everlasting age." Ages may roll on, but the time will never come, when the strength of Messiah's kingdom shall become feeble; when in its weakness it shall give place to one of greater power, and when the Almighty king no longer able to maintain his government, shall be hurled helpless from his throne, and the kingdom purchased by his own blood and established by his own power shall be overthrown, pass away and be among the things that were; for the lips of eternal truth have solemnly declared from the divine pavilion concerning this kingdom, "*it shall stand for ever.*"

And again, Daniel says, chap. vii. 13, 14: "I saw in the night visions, and, behold, one like the Son of man came with the clouds of heaven, and came to the Ancient of days, and they brought him near before him. And there was given him dominion, and glory, and a kingdom that all people, nations, and languages, should serve him; his dominion is an everlasting dominion, which shall not pass away, and his kingdom that which shall not be destroyed." Daniel when favoured with this glorious vision was upon the earth, and the Ancient of days appeared there with him, or near to the earth. One like the Son of man coming in the clouds of heaven, was beyond all doubt the Lord Jesus Christ, returning to earth in like manner as the disciples saw him go, to receive his throne and kingdom: and when he came to the Ancient of days, he gave him that long promised throne and kingdom, the redeemed, the renewed earth, that all nations who dwell thereon should serve him.

The kingdom which the Ancient of days gives to Messiah is represented as universal—comprehending all the nations that dwell on the face of the earth. But while his dominion is declared to be universal—over all people, so is it declared to be everlasting. The kingdom given him by the Ancient of days is not temporary in its duration, for it is affirmed that *it shall not pass away*. The dominion of every monarch who has heretofore reigned in this world, has soon come to an end, thereby showing that his was not the rightful authority, and that it had to give place to another. But when the kingdom is given to Jesus, and the dominion is in his hands, it being his right to reign by divine appointment, by royal headship, by mediatorial purchase, there it will for ever remain. No usurper will be able to dispossess the rightful King whose dominion is maintained by almighty power, and consequently nothing will, nothing can destroy his kingdom. For the honour of his name, and the glory of his majesty it will stand in unshaken strength, in indestructible durability, and while the I AM lives it will continue happy in the bliss inspiring presence of the great KING, and radiant in the ever streaming beams of his cloudless glory. "It *shall not be destroyed*."

The angel Gabriel also declares, the perpetuity of his kingdom and reign when announcing his birth to his mother, when he says, "And he shall reign over the house *of Jacob for ever;* and of his kingdom there *shall be no end*." This declaration of the angel is an epitomized quotation of the prophets and the Psalms, teaching briefly in the clearest manner and the strongest language, the eternal reign and kingdom of Jesus Christ upon the earth. If this language does not teach this important, precious and glorious doctrine, then it may be safely contended, that no language can be constructed that will teach it. If this language does not express endless duration, then there is no language in the Bible that does express it. And if this is not evidence that Christ's government and kingdom shall be eternal, then we have no evidence that anything shall be eternal. Doubts arise, concerning the eternal happiness of believers—the redeemed children of God, and there is no possibility of allaying them, for the very language used to describe their happiness, is used to describe the duration of Christ's kingdom and government, and if the language does not teach that he is to sit upon the throne of his father David, and reign over his kingdom yet to be upon earth *for ever*, neither does it teach that the blessedness of those whom he died to redeem shall be eternal. Since the same language is used to express the duration of Christ's kingdom and reign upon earth, and the duration of the happiness of the redeemed, they stand or fall together.

Other passages teaching the perpetuity of Christ's kingdom and reign upon earth might be cited, but one more shall suffice, Rev. xi. 15: when "the seventh angel sounded, John heard great voices in heaven, saying, 'The kingdoms of this world are become the kingdoms of our LORD, and of his CHRIST; and he shall reign for ever and ever.'" Now if those who uttered the voices in heaven knew what they said, and spake the truth; then they do most positively teach that the kingdoms of this world have to become the kingdoms of Jesus Christ: and that His kingdom established upon the overthrow of these kingdoms shall fill the whole earth; for it is all the kingdoms of the earth that have to give place to His, and that His kingdom which is to overthrow and take the place of all others is to endure eternally: and He in his ever enduring kingdom is to reign for ever and ever. All this and nothing less than all this, the voices which John heard in heaven, do teach and most positively affirm. His kingdom once established upon the earth shall never be overthrown, shall never be succeeded by any other. It abides: it remains: it is eternal.

That Christ then, will establish his kingdom upon earth, and reign for ever and ever in that kingdom, is a doctrine, fully, clearly taught in Scripture. When Christ returns to earth, he comes not to remain for a short or long period: to preside over the solemnities of what is called the judgment day, but to abide for ever. When he establishes his kingdom upon earth it is not to flourish in glory for a season, like ancient or present kingdoms, and then like them to be overthrown, pass away and be succeeded by another. It will be established upon an immovable foundation,—upon the principles of eternal truth and righteousness, upon Immanuel's omnipotent sustaining power, upon the inviolable covenant God made with him, "He shall see of the travail of his soul and be satisfied," yea it will be the kingdom of the restitution of all things:—the new heavens and the new earth to abide before the

Lord for ever, and consequently it shall stand *for ever*; it shall *never* be destroyed."

The most mighty and enduring kingdoms or monarchies upon earth have had their rise, glory, decline and fall. Where is now mighty and far renowned Babylon, with her encircling walls seventy-five feet broad, and three hundred high, with her strong brazen gates and the tower of Jupiter's temple lifting its head nigh seven hundred feet into the clouds, once the glory and sovereign of the world, with her proud boasting Nebuchadnezzar upon the throne, who laid Jerusalem desolate, and led God's people captive at his will? Alas! alas! her beauty, glory, strength,—all have perished and passed away like a vision of the night! Its rock-like fortress, its cloud-capt towers, its gold furnished palaces, where the proud and mighty ones of earth revelled, have all been swept by the besom of destruction, and its strength and magnificence consigned to the dust: and from amidst its ruins where the owl and satyr undisturbed for centuries have played, men are now with laborious industry and thrilling interest digging its ornamental and inscribed stones from the hoary rubbish of antiquity. What have become of the far spreading Persian and Grecian kingdoms which seemed to hold in their strength everlasting endurance? They too, mighty and gigantic, ruling over many lands, have numbered their few days, and passed away like the morning cloud, and their brief existence, and utter desolation, are chronicled only on the page of history. And Rome, "Eternal Rome," "the seven hilled city," once the undisputed mistress of the world, all conquering Rome, that trode with victorious feet over many lands, and for centuries walked in triumph over every dynasty against which she turned her ever victorious arms? What, what has become of that mighty city and empire? Do they stand, do they flourish in unsubdued power and in unfaded beauty still? Ah! no: her strength is gone, her arms are broken, her warrior hosts slain, her sceptre and terror-girt crown in the dust. The blasts of desolation have swept over her, and under them she has crumbled into ruins, and been broken into pieces. All that now remains of her are only the shattered fragments; the enfeebled kingdoms under the scripture designation of the ten toes. And they too, are waiting the rapidly approaching hour of their destruction. The commotions have begun which will become more terrible; the tumults of the nations which will become more wild, frantic, and convulsive, till the coming of the Son of man—till the stone cut out of the mountain without hands, smite these, and with its all-crushing influence, they become small as the chaff of the summer thrashing-floors; and when the terrible crushing work is in progress, and the arm of the Lord is made bare, and His mighty sword of vengeance unsheathed, for the destruction—for the utter annihilation of these kingdoms that stand in opposition to him and the establishment of His all pervading, holy kingdom, the fire for which the heavens and the earth are now reserved will be kindled. These fires will burn, until they have burnt up the works of men, and refined this earth to that purity to which it is the will of God it should be wrought, and then it will emerge from its winding-sheet of flame, and from its shroud of smoke a new creation destined to roll in its orbit for ever. The new earth as after the flood, will then spread its holy bosom beautiful in the eye of God as in the morning of creation, to the genial rays of the sun : its vales enriched with greater fertility and covered with more abundant herbage and flowers ; its mountains clad in more abundant foliage, and it prepared another Eden, for the habitation of the sons of men—the redeemed sons of God, and the Son of God as the lord and king of all crowned with glory and honour at its head, upon this new creation He will establish a kingdom which shall never be moved—never destroyed :—whose power shall never be subdued by the usurping foe, whose might and stability no lapse of years shall shake, but which shall endure in unclouded glory and undiminished strength for ever and ever. That is the kingdom of which God has spoken by the mouth of all His holy prophets since the world began—the kingdom which the God of heaven, the father of the everlasting age, shall set up of which " there *shall be no end* "—" which *shall never* be destroyed."

This everlasting kingdom of our Lord and Saviour Jesus Christ, in which He will personally appear, will be introduced at the commencement of the millennium—at his return to earth. He comes to introduce that kingdom of which there shall be no end, and of which the millennium is the introductory age. The duration of that age is spoken of in scripture as a thousand years; but it can scarcely be supposed that the language used, is to be understood literally, as denoting only a thousand years. If it did, then, Satan would have a far more extended reign upon earth than Jesus Christ. He would have seven thousand years' reign, and Christ would have only one thousand. Nor would the reign of Satan be superior to the reign of Christ, merely as regards time, but also as regards the number of subjects; for those in the one case would certainly be far greater than those in the other: and thus looking at the duration of time, and the superior numbers over whom Satan had reigned, compared with the time and numbers over whom Christ had reigned, it would be difficult to see the force and truth of Paul's declaration, "where sin abounded, grace did much more abound."

But I apprehend that the thousand years, denoting the millennial age, is not literal, but symbolic time. And if this be the case, then each day of the thousand years will denote a year, of Jewish time, three hundred and sixty days, which is the prophetic year, which will make the duration of the millennial age not one thousand years, but three hundred and sixty thousand. This is according to the analogy of prophecy; and what a long age that will be! The human mind is bewildered in contemplating its duration ; it is baffled in endeavouring to compute, or comprehend the number of its years : its almost eternal-like duration. It appears long, long since the creation of the world ; but long as the six thousand years which have well nigh rolled away since the creation of the world may appear, what are they compared with *sixty times* that number—compared with *three hundred and sixty thousand years*, the duration of the millennial age. It stretches away, and away, becoming dimmer and dimmer, amidst excessive glory, until it seems lost in the far remote impervious future—in the refulgent eternity. And looking at this long, long extended age of Christ's glorious and triumphant reign ; and the vast, vast, ever increasing multitudes which will be his loyal and devout servants during that reign, the six thousand years during which Satan has been the god of this world, and the number of the disobedient in whose hearts he has ruled during that period dwindle into littleness, and the truth of Paul's declaration seems gloriously exhibited to view, and amply demonstrated, when he says, " where sin abounded grace did much more abound."

During this long period Christ shall reign the *undisputed* KING over all the nations of the earth. Everywhere his royal, merciful sceptre shall be seen, his imperial power manifest, and the blessedness of his righteous, holy government felt. " Righteousness being the girdle of his loins, and faithfulness the girdle of his reins, His administration will be fraught with the greatest possible benefits and blessings to the subjects of his glorious kingdom, and all nations who dwell upon the earth, in the perpetual enjoyment of these, will call him blessed ; and daily in the gratitude and gladness of their hearts will they praise him. From morning to evening ; from year to year ; from century to century, yea during the long millennial age shall the song of praise, in mingled, melodious unison, go up from all the nations of the earth, like the pure incense of the morning, to the HOLY ONE of Israel upon the throne of his father David—to the KING of kings and the Lord of lords. Satan, the adversary, shut up in the bottomless pit, and prevented from holding men in vassalage vile ; the curse removed under which the whole creation has so long groaned : the earth and the nations of the earth, now ushered into the glorious liberty of the sons of God, under the divinly appointed KING, and him whose right it is to reign, celebrate with rapturous joy their long foretold, their blissful jubilee. Nation, after nation, takes up the strain ; onward and onward the anthems of praise roll, till the untiring song of triumph is echoed round our all joyful globe, and poured from holy tongues in all its sweetness into the ear of HIM, who sits upon the throne of David, and rules over the house of Jacob.

Under the peace and love-inspiring sceptre of the king of righteousness, enmity and animosity, the offspring of the devil, shall wither and die, and be cast out from the human bosom, and the big heart of the earth's converted nations shall swell and throb only with the divine impulses of sincere, strong love, and genuine friendship to each and all the individuals of the universally happy nations. All will see in each a brother, and feel a fraternal affection to that countless brotherhood, strong as the love which burns in the breast to self. Love and friendship will burn in every word, glow in every look, and be embodied in every action, and bind each to all in MESSIAH's own bond of union, and all to himself upon Israel's glorious throne. Dark enmity, fiendish revenge, will not move man to arm himself against his brother ; to plunge the murderous dagger into his heart and stain his hand with his precious blood. Marshalled hosts shall not be seen in furious mortal strife upon the battle-field ; the din of war shall not be heard, nor garments rolled in blood shock the eye ; for under MESSIAH's peaceful reign all nations shall have beaten their swords into ploughshares, and their spears into pruning hooks. Wars unto the ends of the earth have ceased ; the nations are at peace among themselves because the GOD of peace reigns, and by him, through the house of Jacob, the earth enjoys its glorious jubilee. During that prolonged age the nations of the earth with joyful hearts shall come up to Jerusalem, the metropolis of this world, the city of the great KING, to worship and adore him who sitteth upon Israel's throne. Heathenism driven from the earth by the clear shining forth of the knowledge of the

LORD; idolatry overthrown by the visible revelation, the manifest presence of the true God; all religious distinctions and hostilities destroyed, and one faith existing in every bosom; one profession, one practice, one worship observed by all; all men of all nations will flock to the city of the great KING, and honour him with a spiritual and true worship, for then will be fulfilled the glorious prediction, "then will I turn to the people a pure language that they may call upon the name of the LORD to serve him with one consent." Zeph. iii. 9. And this all nations will say with one mind, "Come ye, and let us go up to the mountain of the LORD, to the house of the God of Jacob, and he will teach us of his ways, and we will walk in his paths; for out of Zion shall go forth the law, and the word of the LORD from Jerusalem." Isa. ii. 3.

> "Desire of every land! the nations come,
> And worship at HIS feet; all nations come,
> Flocking like doves * * * *
> * * * * and worship reverently
> Before the LORD on Zion's holy hill."

Israel, too, shall occupy their true position upon the earth and among its inhabitants. They no longer a by-word and reproach, but the peculiar people of the LORD, all nations shall call them blessed. No longer dispersed the earth over with heaven's curse on their head and brand on their brow; but gathered by Jehovah into the land given by him in covenant to Abraham,

Isaac, and Jacob; David's kingdom and throne restored, they shall see the SON of David, their own PRINCE, the HOLY ONE of Israel, sitting upon that throne, chief in that kingdom, bestowing his richest blessings upon them first, and through them upon all the nations of the earth.

During this glorious and blessed reign, when the power of sin and the effects of the curse shall be almost annihilated, the nature of the inferior animals will also be changed. Their savage ferocity, which seemed ever living and ready to destroy, will cease to exist in them, and they will become harmless as doves—their murderous cruelty will be transformed into loviug kindness; their appetite for flesh shall cease, their thirst for blood quenched, and they shall not drink it. The terrible jaws of the lion and tiger and other beasts of prey shall cease to devour and tear the quivering flesh of their victims, and become gentle, harmless as the lamb, and side by side with it, without any desire for its flesh or it having any dread of them, in sweet company crop the flowery food. The fountain of deadly poison dried up in the mouth of the ever hated serpent, and the disposition to bite and deposit the deadly virus in whoever approached him, destroyed; the long existing enmity between him and man shall cease to exist, and they shall live together in love and toying friendship, pleased and delighted with each other. So the prophet in sublime and heavenly strains has sung, "The wolf also shall dwell with the lamb, and the leopard shall lie down with the kid; and the calf, and the young lion, and the fatling together; and a little child shall lead them. And the cow and the bear shall feed; their young ones shall lie down together; and the lion shall eat straw like the ox. And the sucking child shall play in the hole of the asp, and the weaned child shall put his hand in the cockatrice's den. They shall not hurt nor destroy in all my holy mountain; for the earth shall be full of the knowledge of the LORD as the waters cover the sea." Isai. xi. 6–9.

"The wolf and the lambkin together shall meet,
And the leopard repose with the kid at his feet,
And the child shall desport on the hole of the asp,
And the lion shall lead in his infantile grasp.

"For naught shall destroy in the mount of the LORD,
Nor the beast with his fang, nor mankind with the sword,
For the knowledge of God o'er the earth shall be spread,
As the ocean-flood covers its measureless bed."

"The lion, and the libbard, and the bear,
Graze with the fearless flocks; all bask at noon
Together, or all gambol in the shade
Of the same grove, and drink one common stream.
Antipathies are none. No foe to man
Lurks in the serpent now: the mother sees,
And smiles to see, her infant's playful hand
Stretched forth to dally with the crested worm,
To stroke his azure neck, or to receive
The lambent homage of his arrowy tongue."

The groaning earth, too, shall be relieved of its

oppressive burden and ushered into joyful service. Thorns and briers, the fruit of the awful curse in consequence of man's disobedience, which now mar its beauty, and blast and ban its fertility, shall fade and wither away, and the lovely and fragrant plant shall spring up and flourish in beauty where they grew. "Instead of the thorn shall come up the fir-tree, and instead of the brier shall come up the myrtle-tree; and it shall be to the LORD for a name, for an everlasting sign that shall not be cut off;" Isa. lv. 13. Noxious, poisonous weeds which drink up earth's substance, and choke the growth, and cause the death of better and nobler things, and demand daily the consuming toil and the laborious sweat of the husbandman's brow to keep them in subjection, shall have no congenial soil wherein to grow; for the earth renewed will produce only that which is delightful and profitable to man,—" that which is pleasant to the sight and good for food." The curse of sterility repealed, the earth will again, as when it rolled in all its new created goodness from the plastic hand of its Maker, without toilsome labour from the hand of man, almost spontaneously produce its varied and abundant fruits for the supply of its inhabitants. "The earth shall yield her increase, and GOD, even Israel's GOD shall bless the people." The fertile valleys shall then be far more fertile, and the arid wastes, and the sandy deserts where vegetable production had never spread a green leaf to the sun, shall then be converted into a fertile field, like a rich and well watered garden, and shall wave with choicest and abundant fruitage. "The wilderness and the solitary place shall be glad for them, and the desert shall rejoice and blossom as the rose. It shall blossom abundantly, and rejoice even with joy and singing: the glory of Lebanon shall be given unto it, the excellency of Carmel and Sharon; they shall see the glory of the LORD, and the excellency of our GOD."

> "For in the wilderness shall burst forth waters,
> And torrents in the desert!
> And the glowing sand shall become a pool,
> And the thirsty soil bubbling springs;
> And in the haunt of dragons shall spring forth
> The grass, with the reed, and the bulrush."—Isa. xxxv.

"I will open rivers in high places, and fountains in the midst of the valleys. I will make the wilderness a pool of water, and the dry land springs of water. I will plant in the wilderness the cedar, the shittah-tree, and the myrtle, and the oil-tree: I will set in the desert the fir-tree, and the pine, and the box-tree together: that they may see and know, and consider, and understand together, that the hand of the LORD hath done this, and the HOLY ONE of Israel hath created it." Isa. xli. 18–20.

> "Rivers of gladness water all the earth,
> And clothe all climes with beauty; the reproach
> Of barrenness is past. The fruitful field
> Laughs with abundance; and the land, once lean
> Or fertile only in its own disgrace,

Exults to see its thirsty curse repeal'd,
Its various seasons woven into one,
And that one season an eternal spring."

"The desert shall bloom like the rose in its prime,
And the fountains shall gush in the desolate clime,
And the thorn shall give place to the pine-tree of green,
And the myrtle shall flower where the brier-bush hath been."

But great as will be the earth's fertility; and the friendship and happiness that will prevail among its inhabitants; and the holiness of the government which the SON of David will exercise during that glorious dispensation, yet sin, and the effects of the curse will not be entirely removed: the works of the devil will not be completely destroyed. Sin and wickedness will be seen here and there, but they will be so quickly subdued and punished by the holy reigning Prince that their pernicious influence will not be felt in the kingdom. This is clearly taught by Isaiah lxv. 20; "There shall be no more thence an infant of days," or an infant short lived, "nor an old man that hath not filled his days; for the child shall die an hundred years old;" or the individual dying an hundred years old, shall be in age but a child, "but the *sinner* being an hundred years old shall be accursed." Nor is it merely admitted that, during this glorious and blissful age there may be individual sinners among the inhabitants of the earth, like a stray diminutive cloud in the clear vault of heaven; but also, that families may show disloyalty to the Prince of the kingdom, and be disposed to withhold the worship which HE demands, which however by His judgment will soon be reduced to obedience. Zech. xiv. 16—19, "And it shall come to pass, that every one that is left of all the nations which came against Jerusalem shall even go up from year to year to worship the KING, the LORD of hosts, and to keep the feast of tabernacles. And it shall be, that whoso will not come up of all the families of the earth unto Jerusalem to worship the KING, the LORD of hosts, even upon them there shall be no rain. And if the family of Egypt go not up, and come not that have no rain," being watered by the Nile, "there shall be the plague wherewith the LORD will smite the heathen that come not up to keep the feast of tabernacles. This shall be the punishment of Egypt, and the punishment of all nations that come not up to keep the feast of tabernacles." And while there will be thus some wicked men upon the earth; so also will the unholy, cursed dust of the dead bodies of the wicked be mingling with the dust of the earth; and death the last enemy will not be completely destroyed; so that much as sin, and the effects of sin, may be diminished, yet they will not be utterly removed during *that* age of the kingdom.

During the millennial reign there will be three classes upon the earth: CHRIST with his risen and changed glorified saints; the saints in the flesh, and the few sinners that mingle with them. The resurrection, and the changed glorified saints will be immortal, their bodies fashioned like unto Christ's glorious body. "Having been counted worthy to obtain that world," or age, "and the resurrection from the dead; neither marry nor are given in marriage; neither can they die any more; for they are equal unto the angels; and are the children of God, being the children of the resurrection." Their happiness is perfect, it has reached its ever enduring consummation. The law of sin is destroyed in them; their bodies redeemed from corruption and the grave, they trample the vanquished enemy, death, under their feet. They are kings and priests unto God: they are his ministering servants to rule the nations, and occupy in that kingdom high, useful, and responsible stations. The saints in the flesh, or the mortal saints, are they who, during the days of the kingdom, marry and are given in marriage; multiply and replenish the earth. During that age longevity will be greatly increased. The lives of the mortal saints will not be measured by tens but by hundreds of years, as was the life of the antediluvians, for then as the days of a tree, or an oak which may be a thousand years, will be the days of Jehovah's people, and His elect shall long enjoy the work of their hands. They shall not labour in vain, nor "bring forth for trouble" (or generate a short-lived race), "for they are the seed of the blessed of the Lord, and their offspring with them." And during that long lifetime the effects of sin may, and doubtless will be so greatly removed that disease will not affect or afflict the body at all; "the inhabitant shall not say the head is sick or the heart is faint." And then when they come to die life will not ebb away slowly under protracted sickness and severe suffering ; soul and body may and probably will part without a pang. They may die like Moses on the top of Pisgah by the command of Jehovah, or "at the mouth of the LORD," or as the Jews say, "with a kiss from the mouth of the LORD." It is highly probable from the language here used, that Moses died without any suffering ; and so may the saints of God, the blessed of the LORD in the flesh, die in the millennial age. The putting off the body may be to them like the putting off of our garments when we are about to lay ourselves down to repose; and the fear of death will in like manner be taken away, because they will have the unclouded and indubitable testimony that they are God's chosen, sanctified, and beloved ones, and that the spirit stepping out of the body for a season will be attended with no pain and no danger to them, but will only be a transition into higher, greater glory and happiness. And then there is the third class, and a sorrowful class it is—a few sinners in the flesh, still cherishing their enmity against the glorious KING, whose influence will scarcely be felt; who, though they should live to the age of a hundred years, which in that dispensation is but infancy and youth, "shall die accursed."

Such, according to the sure word of prophecy, will be the blessed state of things during the millennial age ;

but when it comes near a close, suppressed wickedness will begin to burst forth, and the KING's holy influence that controlled it being in a great measure withdrawn or suspended, it will spring up in other hearts, and manifest itself more openly, and in more terrible and furious form. Bitter enmity to the Holy Glorious PRINCE, whose gracious and blissful reign, it might have been expected, would have won and secured the love of every heart to himself; which has long been smothered in consequence of his presence and the terrible judgments wherewith he visited its open manifestations, shall begin to burst out wherever it exists, and burn more fiercely according to the time it has been pent up, and the intensity of its suppressed desires to work out its diabolical purposes. Men will manifest a spirit of open rebellion, and meditate the overthrow of the PRINCE of peace, and his glorious kingdom and government; preferring rather to rule in wickedness, than be ruled in holiness—the old satanic feeling coming up in mighty power, rather reign than serve. At this time the seal set upon Satan the arch-deceiver, will be broken by Him who "hath at his girdle the keys of Hell and of death:" the great chain wherewith he has been bound for a thousand years will be loosed, and he will be released from the bottomless pit. Feeling himself once more free, and at large upon the renewed earth where righteousness has long dwelt—raging in awful fury against Him, who so long confined him in the abyss; and having some faint hope of success, and determined upon another desperate trial to vanquish his much hated enemy, the KING who sits upon David's throne: he goes forth into the nations which are in the four quarters of the earth, Gog and Magog, determined upon mighty deeds, upon glorious victory, who in their spirit of enmity, and hatred against Israel's KING, are waiting for his coming. In this state of readiness he appears before them willing and prepared to lead on the battle. Full of enmity—inflamed zeal, he encourages them to engage in the warfare. Their views and his, being in unison, and both earnestly desiring the accomplishment of the same end, they are pleased with him as their leader, and willing to be under his command. At his bidding, and by the working of his mighty power upon the hearts of the children of disobedience, the vast hosts are soon gathered, "the number of whom is as the sand of the sea," and in terrible battle array, the leader and his armies, urged on by desperate fury, and strong but false hopes of victory, hasten up as on eagle wing to Jerusalem, against the LORD the KING, and "compass the camp of the saints about, and the beloved city." Satan rejoices in anticipated slaughter, and cherishes some forlorn, desperate hope that he may yet vanquish the army of Israel, the hosts of the LORD, and see their leader, Jesus of Nazareth fall and die on the battle-field, as he saw Him die on the cross.

But he has performed the last high-handed act of daring rebellion: reached the loftiest summit of satanic wickedness: entered the scene of his final overthrow. The awful moment of his judgment has come, and the ruin which he sought to work upon another, is instantly to be his own. The Omnipotent PRINCE of peace meets him with the whetted sword of destruction in His right hand. Justice stern, righteous, holy, demands the infliction of punishment without one moment's delay. In obedience to her call, the hour having come for her voice being fully heard and regarded, the long insulted MESSIAH pours out His furious wrath upon Satan and his armies; "fire comes down from God out of heaven and devours them;" sweeps them from the earth, casts them out, hurls them in agonizing defeat and multitudinous confusion, into the terrible lake of fire and brimstone which GOD Almighty in righteous indignation prepared for them. His last temptation, act of wickedness, rebellion upon earth has been performed. He is finally and for ever cast out of earth redeemed, renewed, the glorious kingdom of Immanuel, and consigned to the place prepared for him to endure the terrible wrath and vengeance of God ages without end. By this act the GOD-MAN, CHRIST JESUS, destroys the devil. The devil lives, but he lives not to perform acts of wickedness upon the earth; but to suffer eternally in hell under the hand of Jesus, his almighty conqueror, the awful punishment which his wickedness deserves—the retributive vengeance of the LORD.

Satan being thus cast out of the earth, and consigned

to his place of everlasting torment, then comes the second resurrection. All the saints who have died during the millennial age shall be raised from their graves; to be united to those who rose in the first resurrection, and with them inherit the eternal kingdom. This will complete the resurrection of the children of GOD. All, all the bodies, of the redeemed raised from the dead, not one solitary sleeper left behind in the tomb; all fashioned like unto CHRIST'S glorious body, in the rapture of their victory shout with united voice, "O death, where is thy sting? O grave, where is thy victory?"

After the glorious resurrection of the righteous, comes the appalling resurrection of the wicked. By the omnipotent power of GOD, their graves too are thrown open, and reluctant as they may be to leave their dark dwelling-place—shrinking from the terrors of the judgment, and the eternal wrathful retribution awaiting them, they are compelled to come forth. Unwillingly they come, but still, under an irresistible authority *they come.* Omniscience searches them out, and omnipotence brings them forth. Their vile dust, which during the millennial age, mingled with the earth and were "ashes under the soles of the feet of them who feared the LORD;" even that dust which polluted the earth while it remained therein, shall be raised by the power of the Almighty and reconstructed into foul accursed dwelling-places for the impure soul, and brought up for the judgment before the "great white throne," and " HIM that sits thereon." Their names not being found written in " the LAMB's book of life," the sentence of righteous condemnation will be pronounced upon them, and they will be " cast into the lake of fire." Every particle of unholy dust belonging to the wicked will, at their resurrection, be gathered out of the earth ; and at their judgment they will be removed from the earth, and consigned to " the lake of fire ;" so that not one of them shall be found upon the earth. And when all the dead have been raised, then will death the last enemy be destroyed : and when they have been cast into " the lake of fire," then will all the works of the devil be destroyed. Nothing of the devil, or the works of the devil ; neither sin nor sinners will be then seen in the earth ; the times of full, complete, perfect restitution of all things having come.

When all this has been done, the earth will be thoroughly purged from the effects of sin. Nothing impure or unholy will be found thereon, and consequently the curse will be utterly removed. The earth will then be holy as it was when it evolved from the hand of its CREATOR, and when, in His infinite wisdom, He pronounced it " very good." Its inhabitants too will be all holy, for then CHRIST and His redeemed people alone will be upon it. In these redeemed multitudes there is no imperfection, no stain of sin,—they have been thoroughly washed in the blood of the LAMB : they are all arrayed in the spotless robes of CHRIST's righteousness which by faith they have put on. The eye of the HOLY FATHER sees no spot, no wrinkle in them; they are all holy as CHRIST is holy, and in this respect, as well as others, CHRIST and they are one. With Him they are the holy heirs and possessors of the holy earth prepared for them, which is their everlasting inheritance—their eternal kingdom. And now "cometh the end, when He shall have delivered up the kingdom to GOD, even the FATHER, when He shall have put down all rule, and all authority and power."

By the end we are not to understand the end or termination of CHRIST'S kingdom; for of that, the angel Gabriel declared to his mother, "that there shall be no end;" thereby distinctly intimating that *His kingdom would endure for ever.* And the Bible as we have already seen abounds with teaching to that effect. The end here means the last band, the last resurrection company. The subjects of the resurrection are referred to in this, as divided into three bands or companies; CHRIST, the first; they that are Christ's at His coming, the second; and then the wicked who are raised last and at the end of the millennium, the third or last. When they rise, then cometh the last band. The resurrection of the wicked; or of them the last band will be the end, the finishing, the concluding act of that dispensation of the mediatorial undertaking—the finishing of the work at the close of that age which CHRIST engaged to do when He entered into covenant with the Father to redeem this fallen world. The wicked, this last band, having been raised—the work of the millennial age having been finished, and all whom the Father had given Him to be redeemed up to that moment will stand before Him perfect in holiness—stand before Him in His now glorious image fair as Adam in the morning of his creation. The earth too, redeemed, will roll before Him perfect in holiness and laughing in primeval purity, sin and the effects of the curse the fruit of sin as completely removed as if their direful blight and misery had never been seen or felt there ; and Satan cast out, and every trace of him as perfectly removed as if his vile pollution had never marred its new born virgin purity. And now is come the perfecting of the work of redemption, the restitution of all things ; now under the all successful mediatorial management of the LORD JESUS CHRIST, is this earth restored to a condition, holy and happy as that previous to the fall, and the work completed which He covenanted to do.

Whatever may have been the changes wrought upon the earth and its inhabitants at the commencement of the millennium, and during that glorious age of CHRIST'S kingly reign ; and no doubt these will be very great, restoring to a wonderful extent the long lost peace, happiness, and purity ; yet it is not till the end of that age, that the perfect restitution of all things will be accomplished. The close of that age is the last of "times," or the end of the time, for the finishing or perfecting of that work according to what "the holy prophets have spoken." The term *restitution*, signifies the restoring of that which was *taken away*, *forfeited, or lost;* a restoring to a previous or primitive condition, and as used in scripture must mean a restitution of this earth and all things thereon to the same condition, or state in which they originally existed—to the state or condition, in which they were, before man put forth his hand and took of the fruit of the forbidden tree, and his disobedience brought down the curse of God upon himself, the earth, and all therein. And if this be really the meaning of the expression, as there can be no doubt it is, then, "*the restitution of all things*" necessarily involves, and will just be the restitution of the *Paradisiacal state*—the restitution of the earth and its inhabitants to innocence and holiness, and God ruling in all, and all worshipping and glorifying God, He dwelling among men and favouring them with new revelations of His will.

Now we have seen, that at the close of the millennial age, Satan and sin will be cast out of this earth; and that it will be restored to a state of perfect holiness. The earth then, will be holy as it was when it emerged from the waters under the power of the Holy Spirit's wing spread over chaos, and when it rose up in its perfection before the eye of God, and He in smiling approbation pronounced it very good. It will again be the fit and divinely prepared habitation for absolutely holy beings, and the Lord God will not only visit it, as He did Eden of old, but dwell therein.

The saints who have been redeemed during the previous ages of the earth will also be perfect in holiness. Their risen bodies fashioned like unto CHRIST'S glorious body ; they will all in their redeemed state, be in the image of GOD, and be perfectly holy in nature and conduct. They will be as perfectly holy as if they had never sinned, never fallen, and will shine in absolute purity, "as the sun in the kingdom of the Father." These glorious children of the resurrection, "who neither marry, nor are given in marriage," will continue to occupy their own peculiar places, and perform their own peculiar duties, in the offices assigned them by their great Redeemer, during the everlasting age of the kingdom of perfect glory.

But when all this is done, it is manifest, that the restitution is not yet complete—all things are not yet restored. We see not yet upon the renewed earth, all that was upon it, in its unfallen and uncursed state, though there is a near approximation to that blessed order of things. Before Satan in his defection had alighted upon earth's fair creation, Adam and Eve, made in the image of God, walked among the trees and dwelt in the bowers of Eden. In this state of innocence they were immortal ; and GOD'S command to them was, "multiply and replenish the earth." Had they not listened to the voice, and believed the words of the old serpent, "a liar from the beginning ;" they would not have fallen, nor become sinful nor mortal ; they would have multiplied and replenished the earth with pure, holy, immortal beings like themselves; and the image of GOD, which was in the parents, would have been in like perfection in the children; and this they would have done, as long as seemed good in the sight of GOD. And then, their offspring in their turn, would have risen up tò fulfil the high and holy purpose of God, in making man male and female; and thus, the propagation of a holy and immortal race, would have gone on during the ages of eternity. All this, is manifestly implied, in the state in which our first parents were created; and the command GOD gave to them in that state; and had they fulfilled the conditions of the covenant made with them, such would doubtless have been the result: the earth would have been inhabited by an ever increasing, deathless race of holy human beings. But in consequence of Adam's transgression, an entirely different order of things has been introduced. Man, instead of propagating his kind in the image of God, propagates them in the image of the devil; instead of their being immortal,—they are all subject to death. Now, if the "restitution" spoken of in scripture is to be complete, if the works of the devil are to be so destroyed, that the pre-existing order of things shall be perfectly restored, then, there must of necessity appear upon the new earth, *holy beings in flesh,* like Adam and Eve in Eden. And if the abounding redemption which is in Christ Jesus, be adequate to purify those, who have been contaminated by sin; overcome death, bring them up out of their graves, restore them to immaculate holiness, to the perfect image of God, as unquestionably it is, then, beyond all controversy, it is perfectly adequate to take away original sin, or the hereditary taint of the race without subjecting them to death. And if CHRIST, at the close of that age, completely takes away the taint of sin, which all our race have inherited from their great progenitor, it is evident they will be redeemed, they will be made holy, as well as those who were sanctified by the Holy Spirit, under the previous dispensations of ages, and they will be in the *same state*, as were Adam and Eve before their transgression. They will be human beings in the flesh without original sin—holy beings restored to the image of God, and by the restituting merits of the redemption that is in Christ Jesus, as thoroughly restored to the image of God, as Adam and Eve who were made in His image. This being done, then will the restitution of all things designed by God be accomplished; for *then*, upon this redeemed and holy earth, originally designed for the habitation of man, and ultimately created anew for his abode, will be holy beings in the flesh, in the image of God, like Adam and Eve in Paradise. Then this earth and man will be, by the mediatorial undertaking of the Son of God, restored to their primeval condition. That this is the purpose of God, and the ultimate result of the scheme of redemption, is not only clearly deducible from the scheme, and manifestly involved therein, when fully carried out; but seems also distinctly hinted, if not clearly taught in the Bible. And when, the remedial scheme has brought about such gloriously triumphant results, then, will the earth, and its perfectly holy inhabitants, be stupendous monuments to an enraptured creation, of the truth of Paul's declaration, when contemplating this glorious state of things; "where sin abounded grace did much more abound."

Nor will they, who will be the happy subjects of these all perfect and glorious changes having been restored to the unfallen condition of man, be like our first parents in a probationary state. The fact of their restoration prevents the possibility of this. The atonement was made, that they who were redeemed by its merits might abide for ever in that state of blessedness. Like the resurrection and transfigured saints they will be confirmed in holiness; and in this state by the ever-enduring intercession of CHRIST, infallibly remain; for in them, as well as in the others, Emmanuel shall eternally see of the travail of His soul and be satisfied. Like the new earth, created for their everlasting residence; they shall abide before Him, for they are redeemed with an everlasting redemption.

When this everlasting kingdom is established upon the earth in all its perfection and glory, it is said, Isa. ix. 7, "Of the *increase of His government* and peace there shall be no end; upon the throne of David and upon his kingdom; to order it and to establish it with judgment and with justice, from henceforth *even for ever.*"

It is here asserted by the Prophet, in the plainest and strongest language, that of the *increase of the government* of the PRINCE of Peace there shall be no end. Now this prophetic declaration can have only one meaning, namely, that of the increase of the *subjects* of His government, there shall be no end. For if His government is to increase, become greater or more extensive, it can become so *only* by the increase or multiplication, of the subjects over whom it is exercised. During the millennial age it is manifest it will increase rapidly. In that almost sinless dispensation well nigh half the race will not die, and be carried to the grave in infancy, as they are now. Neither will vast multitudes die in the very prime of life, when "their breasts are full of milk and their bones are moistened with marrow;" but in that age the days of God's people "shall be as the days of a tree." They shall live for hundreds of years, and during this almost deathless dispensation, "they shall multiply and replenish the earth" until they become in number "like the stars of the sky and the sand upon the sea shore," and thus will the government of the PRINCE of PEACE increase.

And if His government will thus increase, as doubtless it will, during the millennial age; it is not to be supposed that when *that* dispensation, preparatory to the absolutely perfect and everlasting reign comes to an end, that with it, the *increase* of His government—the *increase* of His subjects will also come to an end; for concerning *that* it is declared, "*there shall be no end.*"

If with the millennium ends the increase of His subjects, then with it also ends the increase of His government. But of the *increase* of his government we are assured there shall be no end, consequently when the millennial age comes to an end the increase of His government still goes on; the subjects of His government continue to multiply, and this increase of the Prince's government, or multiplication of his subjects shall continue for ever and ever. It has been proved that His kingdom, and His kingly government shall be eternal; and it is here asserted that the increase of His government, or of the people over whom HE reigns, shall be cöeval with the duration of His kingdom, and consequently the *increase of His subjects shall have no end*, but shall be eternal. They shall multiply and continue to multiply throughout the flight of endless ages; and according to the number or progress of these ages will be the ratio of increase, the growing multitude of the numbers without number.

When the millennium is introduced we are told that "the God of heaven will set up a kingdom which shall never be destroyed;" and we have seen that one essential part of this never to be destroyed kingdom is the increase of redeemed mankind; and if they cease to increase when the kingdom in the hands of the ROYAL KING attains its perfection, then it is evident, that if the kingdom itself is not destroyed, an important or essential part of the kingdom would be destroyed, namely, the *increase of the subjects*. But there is not a single syllable in the word of God teaching, that the increase of the race shall cease at the close of the millennium, or at any subsequent period; neither is there any plausible ground for such a supposition. If such an idea is entertained it is a groundless assumption, and without any scripture basis whereon to rest. In all the descriptions which we have of the judgment, and of the transactions of that solemn day, there is not *one word* that would seemingly teach, that when it dawns the last human being shall have been born, or come into existence; or that with its opening or closing scenes the increase of mankind shall cease. At the commencement of the millennium, and the personal coming of JESUS CHRIST, the anti-Christian nations will be judged, and the Jews with other nations will be converted, and these with their offspring will be a holy people to the LORD the KING during that glorious age. When it terminates by the final overthrow of Satan, and those that rise in rebellion with him, and the resurrection and final judgment of the wicked, there is no intimation that the increase of Messiah's holy ones shall cease; but on the contrary, that it shall be continued, for of that, "there is to be no end." And why are the wicked finally removed from the earth, but that MESSIAH and His people may inherit it? And why are men in the flesh transformed to perfect holiness, restored to the divine image, yet upon the renewed earth, CHRIST dwelling with them, if they are not to multiply and increase? And if there is to be no end to the increase of his government how are his subjects perpetually to multiply but in this way?

Let no man say that this would be derogatory to men or the race, (not the resurrection saints) transformed into perfect holiness and made immortal, or to CHRIST reigning over them; for the objection would bear with equal force against the very design of TRINITY, in creating man male and female; against the command given to Adam and Eve in innocence; against the Abrahamic covenant; against the incarnation of Christ and the covenant made with him, and against the increase of Messiah's kingdom during the millennial age. If man had never sinned, beyond all controversy, the race would have increased, and never ceased to increase; and no man would ever have supposed it would; and if through the mediation of CHRIST the nations inhabiting the earth at the close of the millennium are restored to perfect holiness—to unfallen purity and immortality, and in that state increase for ever and ever; will any man, in his daring presumption, ascend the throne of judgment, and pass sentence upon the *infinitely wise and holy* GOD, and say of him, when through the redemption of His Son, carrying out his original infinitely wise and benevolent plans, he is acting in a way derogatory to himself, he is establishing and supporting a system of carnality and sensuality? If any should, the judgment is absurd, the sentence is unjust, impious; for these are only the offspring of sin, and can have no existence in a state and among creatures absolutely holy. Nay, if it was worthy of GOD to create man male and female at first, and continue their increase in the way in which he has done in their fallen condition, it is beyond all controversy much more worthy of GOD to continue that increase in their redeemed, restored state in the glorious kingdom, and under the holy reign of the holy KING JESUS. Repudiate this as a carnal kingdom, as a state of things unworthy of God! Men may look upon it as such, but that will not make it what they, in their prejudice and perverse views, would represent it. A carnal kingdom in the common sense of the term it cannot be ; for only holy beings inhabit it, and consequently all their acts are holy ; an absolutely holy BEING reigns over it, and consequently the entire government, and all that is done in that kingdom is holy. Every thing, every act, every event of that holy people and kingdom bears in it, and upon it, GOD'S own inscription, written by his own finger, and exhibited in luminous relief, "HOLINESS TO THE LORD." All do the will and nothing but the will of the LORD ; all serve him and glorify him by every action, and consequently nothing they do is or can be carnal or sensual, but everything pure and holy.

And to this state it might easily be shown that all things under the mediatorial scheme are tending ; and that CHRIST as the Almighty Mediator is, through the merits of his death, working all things into this glorious consummation, and preparing for the holy, endless increase of his government. And for this, special provision, as we have already seen, has been made. Those in the body from whom original sin will be taken away, and perfect holiness and immortality restored by the atonement and intercession of Jesus Christ at the end of the millennium, and the introduction of the perfect state, are they who will multiply the species and thereby increase the government of MESSIAH. The command given to Adam and Eve in innocence will be heard and obeyed, "*multiply and replenish the earth;*" and during that everlasting kingdom of perfection, holiness, and happiness, "the seed of the blessed" will be increasing and rising up before the Lord in absolute holiness of nature. In this state they will continue to multiply without interruption and without end; and in the ever-growing numbers CHRIST will eternally see his perpetually increasing government extending yet more and more; and the number of his offspring becoming yet greater and greater as the cycles of eternity roll on. And in these, as they rise up in countless multitudes before him, he will see the children of the eternal covenant—those whom the Father gave him before the foundation of the world—the purchase of His blood when it was shed on Calvary—the glorious fruit of His own mighty and divine redemption. That age will be peculiarly and emphatically Messiah's "days;" and in these days shall the righteous flourish, not only as regards peace, plenty and happiness, but also as regards the increase of their numbers. And as the eye rolls down the ages of eternity still it can see generation after generation coming into existence to praise the LORD the KING with the song of salvation. And these numbers will, by every revolving age, be increasing like the majestic river, ever becoming greater by its successive tributaries as it sweeps on in its course; and the time will never arrive when it will be said the last one redeemed by the blood of the Lamb has come into existence—the last child of GOD has been born—CHRIST now sees standing before him in living form all that his blood shall save. No, the last shall never come, for "*of the increase of His government there shall be no end.*"

What a glorious and enrapturing view is this! How like GOD, and how worthy of Him; and how far superior to that generally entertained and presented! Men commonly represent the day of judgment as the time when the number saved by the death of CHRIST will be completed. Upon what authority they do this it is difficult to see; for such a doctrine is certainly not clearly taught in scripture; and the question may be fairly propounded to those who hold it, where is it taught? and until the place is designated, the passage pointed out, no great blame can be incurred if assent to such a doctrine be withheld. But if the number of the redeemed be complete at the day of judgment, however great that number may be, it must be small compared with what would be the ever increasing multitude redeemed through the flight of endless ages; it must be stationary, whereas in the other case it would be ever increasing. And if the merits of CHRIST's blood, the efficacy of his atonement be infinite, as unquestionably they are, why should they not be infinitely both as regards time and numbers saving souls? If it should be replied, it is not the will of GOD they should; then, it is but fair, in order to establish this, that the gainsayer point out where this special revelation of GOD's will is made, or prove that such is GOD's will. But as this cannot be done, and the reverse has been done, it is manifest that the number of the redeemed will not be complete at the day of judgment, but will be increasing ages without end.

Nor is this unworthy of GOD, but on the contrary most worthy of Him. If it was worthy of Him to create man at all, and prolong and increase the race after their awful apostasy, surely it cannot be unworthy of Him to prolong and increase the race in their renewed, restituted condition. If it was worthy of Him to redeem some, no matter how great or small the number, for that does not affect the question, surely it is not unworthy of Him to redeem numbers without end, and age after age raise up these to the glory of his grace. On the contrary, so far as finite mind can judge, it is more God-like, more worthy of Him. And if it be as the scriptures clearly teach, the greater the number saved, the greater the glory to GOD and the LAMB, then the ever-increasing number of the saved during the ceaseless flight of ages would add to that glory, and make that work worthy of GOD.

The analogy of nature furnishes a strong argument in favour of the endless increase of the redeemed. It is the law of universal nature, plants and animals, even in their fallen and cursed condition,—" while in subjection to vanity and the bondage of corruption," to propagate their kind, and this they would do ages without end, if not interrupted by the AUTHOR of these laws. But according to the sure word of prophecy, through the atonement of JESUS CHRIST, sin, and consequently the curse, have to be utterly removed ; that all restored to a perfect condition may, in that condition, propagate its kind. And when once restored to that condition is it to be supposed that GOD will arrest the progress, and destroy that which he has already made perfect ; and that, too, when its perpetuity would tend incomparably more to the promotion of his glory ? GOD has for six thousand years been employed in successive creations in this fallen world for his own glory ; and when this earth has been renewed, and converted into the habitation of righteousness and holiness for the increase of pure and holy beings, is it to be supposed that omnipotence will cease its creative work, and that too at the very time when, by its continued operations, God's glory would be more promoted than it had ever been ?

The merit of the atonement, too, seems to argue and demand the endless, infinite progression of the race. If that is infinite and never can be exhausted, why may not an endless succession of beings come into existence to share its benefits? Would not the benevolence of GOD, as well as his ever acting for His own glory, argue powerfully against His fruitlessly treasuring up the merit of the atonement by finally arresting the increase of the human race, and demand the continuance of that increase, that that infinite merit may be exhibited upon an ever increasing scale, in the eternally growing numbers saved thereby to the honour of God's grace, and the ever abounding fulness of the saving efficacy of the great decease which was accomplished at Jerusalem? And would not GOD'S creating beings made holy by the death of His SON, continued for ever and ever, be far more like Him, and the beneficence he has ever manifested, than the contrary, than ceasing to create, and with that the increase of his kingdom ceasing?

This view is also confirmed by scripture, as we have to a certain extent seen. It is declared, "a seed shall serve Him; it shall be accounted to the Lord for a generation. They shall come, and shall declare his righteousness unto a people that shall be born, that he hath done this." All commentators agree that this passage teaches, that in every age there will be some for a generation to the Lord; there will be some born to serve him; and that as they are born his righteousness shall be declared unto them. Let this precious and truthful doctrine be carried out, and it will be found that they, it may be undesignedly, teach the very doctrine contended for, the endless progression of redeemed holy ones. They admit that in the age of the latter-day glory the inhabitants of the earth will be all righteous, all holy, and that in that dispensation there will be a succession of holy generations ; and if this succession has existed for so long a period when or how has it to end? But in their interpretation they impliedly teach, it will never end ; and this is the very doctrine of the passage. It is asserted, " A seed shall serve Him ;" it shall be accounted to the Lord for a, or rather, as it is in the original, for *the generation.* But the word *the generation,* neither itself, nor as it occurs in the passage, signifies a definite number for ever the same ; but an ever increasing number, for it signifies build, pile up, increase, and might have been rendered " a seed shall serve Him ;" it shall be counted to the LORD for the building, piling up, or the increase. And if this be correct, then, while the seed serves Him, the piling up, the adding, the increasing will be progressive ; and if they are to serve Him eternally, so will they be eternally increasing. And this eternal increase or progression will furnish them with the perpetual opportunity of declaring the Lord's righteousness unto a people that shall be born from generation to generation through the flight of endless ages. This seems to be the doctrine taught in this passage. Look at the generation then, the holy ones inhabiting the new earth, and from that generation we are taught, a new generation shall spring up to serve the LORD, and so on eternally, each declaring to the other his righteousness ; for surely it will not be contended, that when the generation, or the increasing, inhabiting the earth become all holy, the Lord will cut off their increasing, and their service to Him of declaring his righteousness to a people that shall be born, when he has declared that they and their offspring with them shall inherit the earth for ever and ever.

The same doctrine seems further taught by the sweet singer of Israel, Ps. cii. 25–28, " Of old hast THOU laid the foundation of the earth, and the heavens are the works of thy hands. They shall perish, but THOU shalt endure ; yea, all of them shall wax old like a garment ; as a vesture shalt THOU change them, and they shall be changed ; but THOU art the same, and THY years shall have no end. The *children of* THY servants shall continue, and *their seed* shall be established before Thee." Here reference is made to the change through which the earth and the heavens or surrounding atmosphere are destined to pass ; and it is asserted, that amidst all these changes Jehovah shall remain unchanged. " Thou art the same, and Thy years shall have no end." When the new heavens and the new earth have been created, Jehovah Jesus will live eternally in them. But if He is to survive these changes, and live years without end, so also are his redeemed people for whom this new creation " is prepared. The children of thy servants shall continue, and their seed shall be established before thee ;" that is, while CHRIST continues to exist they shall continue ; for they and their seed are to continue, or dwell, or be established before him. This establishing takes place at the time of the new creation, and when introduced into this state they are to increase; and if that increase once begin, where and when shall it end? End it can have none; like the abiding of his servants before Him it will continue for ever; it will be established as an order in the kingdom, and their numbers will be perpetually increasing. If it ends, then also may the continuance of the children of his servants before him end. The increase of the race seems clearly implied both here and elsewhere. "He shall see his seed. He shall *prolong his days*, and the pleasure of the LORD shall prosper in his hand." "Of the *increase* of his government there shall be no end."

The same doctrine is not only implied, but manifestly taught in the covenant made with Abraham. He and his seed are to have the land for an everlasting possession; and when in possession of that land, the LORD promised to multiply his seed as the stars of heaven. Abraham and his seed have never yet inherited the land; nor have his seed been so multiplied; but when they are gathered from the lands whither GOD in His anger has driven them, according to His sure word of promise, and united under one head, under God's servant, the Beloved, then will they begin to multiply, and having once begun, where in scripture is it taught, or even insinuated, that they shall ever cease to multiply? Man may assert they will, at the day of judgment; but it has already been shown, that that is the time when they will increase more rapidly; and therefore, the reason of the assertion is demanded. Men may take it for granted, that the increase of the race will cease at the day of judgment or at some other epoch, but as such a doctrine is not taught in the Bible, proof upon this point is demanded. When the seed of Abraham get the promised land for an everlasting possession, they will consist of parents and children, and the getting possession of the inheritance, will not surely prevent the children growing up to manhood; neither will it prevent them from multiplying. On the contrary, it is when they have possession of the land, that the LORD has promised to make their number as the stars of the sky, and the sand upon the sea shore. And if they are to possess the land for ever; and if, when entering upon the possession of the land, to increase in numbers; and that too, for ages after ages, why are they not in the eternal possession of the land to increase for ever? The land was promised to them for an *everlasting* possession, that they might *for ever multiply* in the land: and it would be as consistent to hold, that they shall not have that land for an everlasting possession, though GOD has sworn they shall, as, that they shall not as long as they possess that land multiply therein.

Moreover, the promise to Abraham in the covenant, was, "In blessing, I will bless thee, and in multiplying, I will *multiply thee.*" Now it will not be denied, that in this promise, God intimates to Abraham that He will bless his seed eternally; and if this be true and admitted, then it must also be true and admitted that He will multiply his seed eternally. There is no intimation that the work of blessing them is perpetual, and the work of multiplying them only temporary. God's blessing them and God's multiplying them according to the very nature of the covenant and promise, must be, and assuredly are co-enduring. If then He blesses them eternally, as assuredly He will do, as certainly will He multiply them eternally. The continuance of blessing and the multiplying stand or fall together.

The *ceaseless* propagation of the race, is also taught by the angel Gabriel, when he declared to His virgin mother, "He shall reign over the house of Jacob for ever, and of His kingdom there shall be no end." When the restored throne of His father David is given to Him, and according to the promise and prophecy, He begins to reign over the house of Jacob; we have seen, that the Jews are to be converted, and multiply under His divine and holy government. Of this there can be no doubt, for it is clearly taught in scripture. Now it is the introduction of this kingdom, that is to bring about this order of things; but this kingdom when once introduced is to be eternal: "He shall reign over the house of Jacob *for ever*, and of His kingdom there *shall be no end*." Now it cannot be supposed, that it is merely of the continuance of the government or rule, or of the duration of the kingdom itself, that there shall be no end; but also, of the *increase* of the subjects of the kingdom. The increase of the human race is a part of the government and kingdom, and is indeed an essential part; and if, of the kingdom and government there is to be no end, neither is there to be of that important part, the *increase* of the human race, which is elsewhere designated the increase of the government, and of which it is affirmed there shall be no end.

This might have been farther argued from the eternity of Christ's priesthood; from His perpetual intercession; from His ability to save to the uttermost of time—the uttermost of the eternal ages, them that come unto God by Him: the perpetuity of the earth, and other things appertaining to the kingdom: but we forbear. We have seen from the analogy of creation: from the merits of CHRIST's atonement; and from the teaching of *God's* word, that Messiah's kingdom will be eternal: and that the human race restored to perfect holiness, will in that eternal kingdom endlessly increase. How glorious the thought! How worthy of GOD that order of things! Through the light of revelation, we see Jesus Christ returning to this earth, "in like manner as the disciples saw him go,"—coming in the clouds of heaven with power and great glory, and the ten thousand times ten thousand of His saints, and all His holy angels with Him. The voice of the archangel and the trump of GOD, pours from amid the glory covered heavens, rolling round the globe—in its progress opening the graves and breaking the slumbers of God's holy ones reposing in the tomb ; and under its mighty power "these mortals put on immortality ; these corruptibles put on incorruption"—their bodies everywhere arise from the earth, and the ocean's dark wave, and as they come, successively come in vast multitudes, "are fashioned like unto Christ's glorious body," sitting on the white cloud, and the living believing ones are changed. The Jews, and others are converted, and become the holy inhabitants of earth. "The groans of this creation cease, being delivered from the bondage of corruption into the glorious liberty of the sons of God"—the long waited for adoption,—the resurrection of the body having come. The inferior animals dwell together in harmony, the ferocity of their nature being destroyed. The earth everywhere becomes fruitful as the garden of the LORD, and the holy and happy children of GOD inhabit it. Ages in endless succession roll on, and generation after generation without end, rise up under the perpetual government of JESUS CHRIST sitting for ever upon the throne of His father David, to the increase of His government, to the glory of His grace ; and to swell the rapturous anthems of His praise. Amid all, above all, we see the Son of the virgin, the God-Man enshrined in glory, moving in glory, and an universe of glory and happiness moving around Him, and as the eye labours to look yet farther into the dazzling abyss of eternity, that already inconceivably great glory seems brightening, increasing ; and generation after generation, of pure and holy beings appear coming into glorious existence; each successive one surpassing in number the preceding; and the enravished ear listens with ecstasy to the song of praise, ever becoming more majestic in its perpetually increasing swell, as the eternal generations come and lift up their voices in that universal song.

Reader, that kingdom of boundless, endless glory is before you. It has been revealed in GOD's holy word to attract your attention, to captivate your heart, to call forth your energies to obtain it. The SON of GOD has been "made of a woman, made under the law"—He has become man,—He has agonized in the garden, bled, died upon the cross, descended into the tomb that you might inherit and enjoy this kingdom endless, boundless in glory and happiness. Now will you accept of this kingdom as your everlasting inheritance? You are upon earth at this moment for settling this grand, this awful question. This is *the* business, the important, the whole, the sole business of life. You are here on earth, really for no other purpose than to settle this question; than to choose or reject this kingdom. You may think you have other business, but assuredly you have not; for whatever you may think you have, it is not the small dust of the balance when weighed against this—it is lost—utterly lost—annihilated in the overwhelming, immense importance of this. You are here to determine the question, and the time allowed for the decision is very short, and every moment becoming shorter ; and the hour is at hand—Oh ! methinks I hear the solemn warning of its coming knell, when, if not having decided to accept the kingdom, it will be lost—lost for ever. One moment's delay in cordially accepting it—in grasping it with the hand of faith, and it may be beyond your reach ; and all the agonizing regrets which can wring the heart, and all the fervent prayers which the lips can utter, will not restore that lost opportunity. Ah ! no. *Now*, and only now, is the time to decide, the time to accept. The spirits of the Old and New Testament saints are a cloud of witnesses hanging over your head, waiting for your decision ; angels are waiting for your decision ; and the LORD JESUS CHRIST has spared you to this moment, that you might make a decision, and He is waiting for it. He points you with one hand to the place of outer darkness—to the lake that burns with fire and brimstone ; and with the other to that kingdom whose glory shall never fade, whose happiness shall never end, and says to you which will you choose for your everlasting portion ? and waits for your answer. *He waits.* And can you hesitate, do you hesitate in such a situation as this ? Hesitate, when the salvation of the soul is at stake ; when the kingdom of eternal glory and happiness is the prize ! Hesitate, when the end of hesitation may be,—certainly will be, if persisted in, eternal damnation. Oh ! choose the kingdom, the blood-bought, the redeemed, the glorious kingdom this very moment, and you shall eternally move among the sons of God, shine in the glory that emanates from the Lamb, and triumph in the ever abounding joy of his presence: but if you postpone it *one moment*, then, it may be too late; and then, Oh, fearful thought! you will sink, sink, sink eternally amid "the unquenchable flames of that lake which burns with fire and brimstone."

CHAPTER IV.

THE TIME WHEN THE KINGDOM SHALL BE GIVEN TO MESSIAH.

"The Lord God shall give unto Him the throne of His father David; and He shall reign over the house of Jacob for ever; and of His kingdom there shall be no end."—LUKE i. 32, 33.

WE have seen Messiah's throne and kingdom to be a literal throne and kingdom, as literal as any of the ancient thrones and kingdoms that ever existed upon earth. We have glanced at the extent of that kingdom, and seen that it is to consist not only of the land of Canaan given in covenant to Abraham, Isaac, and Jacob, but of the whole earth—that all other kingdoms are to give place to it—that the kingdoms of this world, or the territory whereon they exist, have to become his kingdom. "He shall reign from sea to sea, from the river unto the ends of the earth." We have glanced also at the perpetuity of his kingdom, and seen, when it is introduced, set up or established upon the renewed earth, it will exist in millennial glory not merely for a thousand years, but for three hundred and sixty thousand. And when this period of the kingdom of great glory comes to a close, and which is but introductory to yet greater glory; every thing unholy will be removed from earth and its inhabitants; all will be wrought by the purifying merits of the great decease which was accomplished at Jerusalem into perfection, holiness, and glory, and in this state continue for ever and ever. We come now to glance for a moment at *the time when* this kingdom shall be given unto the SON of the Highest and he shall sit upon the throne of his father David.

The Holy Scriptures frequently, and by various events, clearly describe the time and mark out the epoch when the throne of his father David and the government of the earth shall be given to PRINCE MESSIAH. It would be pleasing and profitable withal, to advert to the numerous passages in the Bible and examine those that refer to the *time* when this kingdom shall be given to Jesus; but a few, and only a few must suffice. And at these we shall give only a passing glance.

The *time when* the kingdom shall be given to Messiah is clearly pointed out in Dan. vii. 7–28. "After this I saw in the night visions, and behold a fourth beast, dreadful and terrible, and strong exceedingly; and it had great iron teeth; it devoured and brake in pieces, and stamped the residue with the feet of it; and it was diverse from all the beasts that were before it; and it had ten horns. I considered the horns, and, behold, there came up among them another little horn, before whom there were three of the first horns plucked up by the roots; and, behold, in this horn were eyes like the eyes of man, and a mouth speaking great things.

"I beheld till the thrones were cast down, and the Ancient of days did sit, whose garment was white as snow, and the hair of his head like the pure wool: His throne was like the fiery flame, and his wheels as burning fire. A fiery stream issued and came forth from before Him; thousand thousands ministered unto him, and ten thousand times ten thousand stood before him; the judgment was set, and the books were opened. I beheld then, because of the voice of the great words which the horn spake; I beheld, even till the beast was slain, and his body destroyed, and given to the burning flame. As concerning the rest of the beasts, they had their dominion taken away; yet their lives were prolonged for a season and time.

"I saw in the night visions, and, behold, one like the Son of man came with the clouds of heaven, and came to the Ancient of days, and they brought him near before him. And there was given him dominion, and glory, and a kingdom, that all people, nations, and languages, should serve him: His dominion is an everlasting dominion, which shall not pass away, and his kingdom that which shall not be destroyed.

"I Daniel was grieved in my spirit in the midst of my body, and the visions of my head troubled me. I came near unto one of them that stood by, and asked him the truth of all this. So he told me and made me know the interpretation of the things. These great beasts, which are four, are four kings, which shall arise out of the earth. But the saints of the Most High shall take the kingdom, and possess the kingdom for ever, even for ever and ever. Then I would know the truth of the fourth beast, which was diverse from all the others, exceeding dreadful, whose teeth were of iron, and his nails of brass, which devoured, brake in pieces, and stamped the residue with his feet; and of the ten horns that were in his head, and of the other which came up, and before whom three fell; even of that horn that had eyes, and a mouth that spake very great things, whose look was more stout than his fellows. I beheld, and the same horn made war with the saints, and prevailed against them; until the Ancient of days came, and judgment was given to the saints of the Most High; and the time came that the saints possessed the kingdom. Thus he said, the fourth beast shall be the fourth kingdom upon earth, which shall be diverse from all kingdoms, and devour the whole earth, and shall tread it down, and break it in pieces. And the ten horns out of this kingdom are ten kings that shall arise; and another shall rise after them; and he shall be diverse from the first, and he shall subdue three kings. And he shall speak great words against the Most High, and shall wear out the saints of the Most High, and think to change times and laws; and they shall be given into his hand, until a time and times, and the dividing of time. But the judgment shall sit, and they shall take away his dominion, to consume and to destroy it unto the end. And the kingdom and dominion, and the greatness of the kingdom under the whole heaven, shall be given to the people of the saints of the Most High, whose kingdom is an everlasting kingdom, and all dominions shall serve and obey him. Hitherto is the end of the matter."

The fourth beast in this magnificent group of symbols symbolizes the Roman power, that great monarchy as it existed at the time, and after conquering the Grecian Empire. The ten horns symbolize the monarchies or kingdoms into which it was subsequently divided, which still exist; but which are now trembling before the prelusive commotions of the fast-coming tempest of certain and awful destruction. The little, or eleventh horn, having eyes, and the mouth speaking great things, symbolizes the papacy, and the mighty power exercised by it. By the thrones being cast down or set, and the Ancient of days sitting, is evidently meant the day of judgment. The language here used can apply to nothing else; and it is the language commonly used to describe the coming of the Judge and the scenes of that day; and this is its acknowledged meaning. The one like the SON of man is acknowledged by all commentators to be the Lord Jesus Christ; and this is the title given to Him and the title which he assumes in the New Testament. His coming with the clouds of heaven denotes his coming to judgment; for this is the very language in which he and his disciples describe his return to earth—His coming on that day. "He will come in the clouds of heaven with power and great glory." And when he thus comes, according to the vision, there are given him everlasting dominion and glory and a kingdom, that universal service and homage may be rendered to him. Now this distinctly teaches that he is to be the supreme and universal sovereign of earth; for all people, nations, and languages are to serve him. These only exist upon the earth, and compose that kingdom of which he is to be the Monarch. Now these powers indicated by these symbols are to exist till the day of judgment—till the thrones are cast down—till the Son of man comes for their destruction, and the introduction of his own kingdom; consequently, the time of the destruction of these kingdoms is *the time* of the coming of the Son of man: and the time of his coming *is the time* when the kingdom is given to him. The second beast, the Medo-Persian monarchy, destroyed the first beast, the Babylonian monarchy; the third beast, the Grecian monarchy, destroyed the Medo-Persian; the fourth beast, the Roman monarchy, destroyed the third; and now the fourth, or Roman monarchy, as certainly foredoomed to destruction as those that preceded it waits its destruction, and the heavens and the earth are full of the portentous signs of its rapid coming and near approach; and that is to be done by the smiting of the stone cut out of the mountain without hands—by the coming of the Son of man in the clouds of heaven—by the second advent of Jesus Christ. When he comes then he destroys that monarchy and establishes his own, just as each of the preceding monarchies had done. No kingdom, no reign intervenes between the destruction of the fourth beast, the Roman dynasty, and the kingdom of Messiah. When that kingdom, then, is destroyed by CHRIST'S coming he receives his kingdom, *the whole earth.* The time of his coming then, and the destruction of these monarchies, *is the time when* he shall receive his kingdom.

Further, Daniel distinctly specifies the duration of the Papacy or anti-Christian power—how long it shall wear out the saints of the Most High. They shall be given into his hand, "until a time and times, and the dividing of time;" which is according to the usual interpretation twelve hundred and sixty years. When this time expires he affirms, the judgment shall sit, that is the great Judge of the earth shall occupy the throne of judgment—arraign his enemies before him—pronounce the righteous sentence of condemnation upon them—inflict upon them the punishment they deserve, and destroy him and his power who destroyed the saints. This day of judgment and retributive justice will take away him who spake great swelling words against the Most High, and did wear out his saints, and will take away his dominion to consume and destroy it unto the end. And when all this destruction is accomplished upon that anti-Christian power, then will the kingdom under the whole heavens, which shall have no end, be given to Jesus Christ and his saints. The time then, when the judgment sits—when Antichrist, the persecuting power, is destroyed, and his kingdom utterly consumed, *is the time when* the kingdom is given to Messiah.

Many other passages, from the prophets and the book of Revelation, specifying in like manner the time when the kingdom shall be given to Jesus, might be adduced and examined ; but it is deemed unnecessary. In perfect accordance, however, with all this, is the teaching of Paul in 2 Thess. i. 8, " And then shall the wicked be revealed, whom the Lord shall consume with the breath of his mouth, and shall destroy with the brightness of his coming." That wicked, and the person in the third verse designated the man of sin, is evidently one and the same person. It is admitted by all commentators, that these names denote Antichrist. Mention is made of an epoch when he shall be fully revealed—revealed in all his power ; and when that time comes, when that full revelation is made, or when he is exercising and working in the mightiness of his power, then the LORD JESUS CHRIST will consume him with the breath of his mouth, and destroy him with the brightness of his coming. But this destruction is to be accomplished at, and by the Lord's glorious coming. And the glorious coming here spoken of, is the glorious coming of the Lord Jesus Christ to this earth for judgment as is clearly taught in the preceding part of the chapter ; consequently the time when the destruction of " that wicked," "the man of sin," takes place *is the time* when Messiah receives the kingdom and sits down upon the throne of his father David.

Again, *the time when* the Jewish nation shall be converted to the faith and public acknowledgment of Jesus of Nazareth as their Messiah, *is the time*, when His kingdom shall be set up and established upon the earth, as is clearly implied in His own words; "Henceforth ye shall not see me until ye shall say, Blessed is He who cometh in the name of the Lord." Christ who possessed the gift of prophecy, yea, was omniscient, and saw clearly all the actions of all generations yet unborn, gave the Jews whom He addressed, distinctly to understand that He was about to leave them, and the earth whereon they dwelt. He intimated at the same time, that His absence *would* be only temporary, and that He would return, and that they would see Him again. But upon His next appearance, or return to earth, they would not brand or reject Him as an impostor; they would not refuse to recognise Him as the long expected Shiloh. As a nation with eyes unscaled, and vision divinely illuminated they would see His true and glorious character, and with hearts throbbing with ecstasy at His coming, they would recognise, and hail Him with the most rapturous hosannas as their PRINCE OF PEACE. That divinely predicted advent or return has not yet taken place; the heavens yet retain the King of the Jews, and the land of Israel has not yet echoed with the greetings of their King; but He will return as certainly as He uttered these words and left them. As certainly as they saw Him, and rejected Him, as certainly shall they in a national capacity see, and receive Him with the most rapturous joy. The time of His return, then, and public and national reception, *is the time*, when the kingdom shall be given to him;—when He shall assume the government of which the prophets have spoken—restore the kingdom to Israel, and sit upon the rebuilt throne of His father David, and reign over them, and through them over the whole earth, His own, entirely His own kingdom in righteousness for ever and ever.

That the kingdom shall be given to Christ at the time of the national restoration and conversion of the Jews, is also clearly taught by Peter in Acts iii. 19, when addressing the murderers of the Lord, and charging them with the awful sin of crucifying the Prince of life, he says, "Repent ye, therefore, and be converted, that your sins may be blotted out, so that the times of refreshing shall come from the presence of the LORD; and He shall send Jesus Christ, who before was preached unto you: whom the heaven must receive until the times of restitution of all things, which God hath spoken, by the mouth of all His holy prophets since the world began." The grand doctrine clearly taught in this passage is, that when the Jews nationally repent of crucifying the Lord of glory, and recognise JESUS of Nazareth, as their Messiah, the times of refreshing will come; that is, GOD's covenant blessings promised to the fathers will be conferred upon them in all their fulness. Jesus Christ shall be sent to them as their KING—their glorious reigning Messiah, to terminate "the groans of nature in this nether world which heaven has heard for ages:" to restore all things made subject to vanity, suffering, and desolation by him who hath subjected the same in hope, to restore the kingdom to Israel, and reign in righteousness over a redeemed earth, of which all the prophets have spoken since the world began; which will be the restitution of all things—the fulness and brightness of the latter-day glory—the millennial dispensation, for which the souls under the altar are crying—the spirits around the throne looking forward, and even we ourselves groaning within ourselves. Now the time of the national conversion of Israel, is *the time*, when the refreshing shall come from the presence of the LORD, and all these glorious things shall be accomplished. But that time is the *time* when Messiah shall return, as is clearly taught in the passage, and consequently, *the time* when He shall receive the kingdom.

That the kingdom shall be given to Christ at this epoch is equally clearly taught by Paul, Rom. xi. 25, 26. "For I would not, brethren, that ye should be ignorant of this mystery (lest ye should be wise in your own conceits), that blindness in part is happened to Israel, until the fulness of the Gentiles be come in. And so all Israel shall be saved: as it is written, There shall come out of Zion the Deliverer, and shall turn away ungodliness from Jacob." The blindness and rejection of Israel is temporary, namely until the fulness of the Gentiles be come in. When the time for bringing in the fulness of the Gentiles has expired, and when that great and glorious work shall have been accomplished, *then*, the blindness of Israel shall be removed:—they shall see Messiah in His person, in His true character, and as cordially embrace Him as their fathers rejected Him. And this great and glorious work shall be accomplished by the Deliverer, the Son of David himself; for then He is to come out of Zion and turn away ungodliness from Jacob. When He does this He is upon the earth, and the time of His doing this, is *the time when* He receives the kingdom. It is as the king already in possession of the kingdom, having supreme and universal power in His hands, that He comes out of Zion the metropolis of His kingdom, and turns away ungodliness from Jacob, and through the house of Jacob exercises His royal rule over all the nations of the earth.

Contemporaneous with all this is the fulfilment of the times of the Gentiles. When their times are fulfilled, Jerusalem which was laid in ruins and desolation by them, and has been for centuries, and now is, trodden down by them, shall be rebuilt. Israel's long scattered, oppressed, weeping children shall return from the many lands of their exile, to do this work most vehemently desired by every heart. The Lord himself will prepare their way, and help them in the glorious undertaking. "Thou shalt arise, and have mercy upon Zion; for the time to favour her, yea, the set time is come. For thy servants take pleasure in her stones, and favour the dust thereof." When the times of the Gentiles are fulfilled, Jerusalem shall be rebuilt, as the city of the Great King, and the throne of David rebuilt in it, for the occupancy of that glorious king; and, *then*, God's covenant and promise will be fulfilled; for *then*, He will set the seed of David according to the flesh upon that throne, and give Him the nations of the earth for His inheritance, and the uttermost parts of the earth for His possession. The Psalms, and the Prophets, and the Epistles and the Apocalypse all point out that as the time, when the kingdom shall be given to PRINCE MESSIAH, the Son of the Highest. They point out also, the resurrection of the righteous dead: the day of judgment, and the time of other events, to which we deem it unnecessary to refer, and with which every attentive reader of the Bible must be familiar, as *the time* when the kingdom shall be given to Jesus Christ.

Now if all this be correct; and it surely does appear to be the plain and uniform teaching of scripture, then, Antichrist will not be destroyed till the time of the Jews' conversion—till the time of the Gentiles be fulfilled: or, in other words, till the Lord come, and cast the beast and false prophet into the lake of fire prepared for the devil and his angels; and bind Satan and shut him up, and take the kingdom to Himself. If Antichrist be not destroyed till then, and scripture does not teach he shall be, but that he shall not be; and if the latter-day glory cannot be ushered in till Anti-christ is destroyed—till she who has drunk the blood of the saints, and is still ready to drink it, is utterly consumed by the devouring fire: nor the meek—the saints possess the earth, then, it unavoidably follows, that, the cry cannot be heard, "The kingdoms of this world have become the kingdoms of our Lord, and His Christ." Or, in other words, there can be no millennium till the Lord himself come to sit upon the raised up throne of His father David; and to set up and establish that kingdom of glory and blessedness, "for which the whole creation is groaning and travailing in pain together."

That the latter-day glory of the church will not be ushered in till the same Jesus, who was taken up into heaven, shall return in like manner as the disciples saw Him go, might be argued from the whole tenor of scripture. But suffice it to say, that the latter-day glory of the church is the time to which patriarchs, prophets, disciples, apostles, martyrs and godly men in every age have looked forward with the deepest interest; and in describing that, prophecy has poured forth her loftiest strains—her most enraptured and glowing descriptious: and, surely, if that dispensation had to be ushered in by the preaching of the gospel, as it is preached in these days—had to exist upon the earth previous to the coming of the Son of man, and immediately precede his advent, it might have been expected that he would have mentioned that to his disciples as one of the signs; and the most important sign of his coming. It might have been expected that among the signs which he mentioned this would have its own prominent and conspicuous place; that he would have said, the gospel shall be preached among all nations—all men shall believe, and holiness and blessedness, righteousness and peace embracing each other, shall reign a thousand years upon earth previous to my coming. But the latter day glory of the church—the millennium holds no place among the signs mentioned to intimate the LORD's coming, and, therefore, the conclusion is, that the millennium will not precede the second advent of the SON of man; but according to the uniform teaching of Scripture, and particularly the twentieth chapter of Revelation, will be introduced by his coming, and perpetuated by his presence and righteous government, when he shall sit upon the throne of his father David. "The LORD of hosts shall reign in mount Zion and in Jerusalem, and before his ancients gloriously." The time then, when Christ returns to earth, destroys his enemies, raises the saints from their graves, converts the nations, introduces the millennium, is *the time when* the kingdom shall be given to him.

But while the time is thus pointed out by the concurrence of such a multiplicity of events, a question naturally arises, What is the probable date of the kingdom being given to Messiah? In speaking upon this point caution is necessary, in consequence of the different results in the calculation; and the consequences that have followed because of the inaccuracy of these calculations. Every person in these days is familiar with the mistakes of the pious and zealous Mr. Miller; with the confidence he manifested in the accuracy of his calculations respecting the advent of the great God and Saviour; and the unhappy results that followed when the Lord Jesus did not come at his computed time. If his eye had not been so fixed upon dates that he could see nothing else—could not discern the signs of the times, he would not have made such unhappy mistakes. At the very time he was proclaiming the year of Messiah's return to earth with such confidence over the land; and his fanatical followers preparing with such industry and zeal their ascension robes, as they were foolishly called, and of which the scriptures know and teach nothing; we maintained he was mistaken, simply because the signs of the times were not fully developed nor fulfilled; the great convulsions among the nations had not taken place; the prophetic doom of the toe kingdoms had not come, nor the predictions concerning the Jews been fulfilled. The preceding and contemporaneous events, as foretold by the Hebrew prophets, must coincide with the date; must have their fulfilment according to their order before and at the time of the date; but as these predicted events immediately preceding the Lord's return in the clouds of heaven, were not being fulfilled, the inevitable and correct conclusion, as time has shown, was, that Mr. Miller was certainly in error as regards dates.

The events that are to transpire—the convulsions that are to take place among the nations, especially among those symbolized by the ten-horned beast, seem to have begun and be in rapid progress. The explosive materials have been laid, the fuses arranged, and in many instances the hand seems approaching with the match; and the touch may soon be given which will convulse the whole and place them in the very position in which prophecy declares they shall be at the coming of the Son of man. All this may be done, and prophecy by the time which it mentions, by the dates which it gives, and the events which it reveals and declares shall precede and occur at the coming of the Son of man favours the opinion and the calculation, that all this will be done in the short time of about twelve years. According to the calculations of many, the Son of man will return to earth about the year 1866, and then the kingdom will be given to him. In common with many others the talented author of the pamphlet entitled, "The Coming Struggle of the Nations of the Earth," holds this opinion. He seems profoundly instructed in the prophets, and to see with peculiar clearness the movements and destiny of the nations, the struggle through which they have to pass, the coming of Messiah; the destruction of the Wild Beast and his armies; the introduction of the millennial kingdom, and the giving of the kingdom to the Son of man by the

ANCIENT of days, and is therefore well worthy of careful perusal. By seemingly correct calculations, he makes it appear that twelve years hence, or in the year 1866, the glorious kingdom will be given to Messiah, and then he, with his saints, will possess the earth—the kingdom and the greatness of the kingdom under the whole heavens.

TWELVE YEARS! How *short* a time is twelve years; and yet how *long* to that servant waiting for the coming of his Lord! and crying in sincere desire, "Come, LORD JESUS, come quickly." Glorious event; the glory of all that is glorious! Rapturous day, if we really love the Lord and his appearing! Who can anticipate that day without the most thrilling emotions, without looking for it with the most vehement desire? The thought, the anticipation of that day make believers in Jesus madmen, and fit only for the cell of the Lunatic Asylum! Ah! then may the thought—the anticipation of the coming bridegroom to the much desired nuptials by her waiting for him, make the bride a maniac; disqualify her for the matrimonial life and send her to live and rave with insanity! Away, away with such misrepresentation and blasphemous lies. As soon might the thought of seeing and meeting the Saviour in Paradise after death make the dying Christian a maniac and send him raving in madness into eternity—as soon might the thought of seeing him at the day of judgment, which is precisely the same thing, produce such results—produce insanity. No, no. The thought of the coming of the SAVIOUR, the LORD, the KING being near, being twelve years hence, to-morrow, or even to-day, will never make genuine, humble believers madmen. Oh! it is this very event they desire—this very event they are waiting and praying for—the very event for which they are groaning within themselves; and when they realize its nearness *shall they become maniacs?* If they do by anticipation what will be their condition—what their madness when the glorious sight is revealed and they actually see JESUS coming in his own and his Father's glory? We shrink from such a thought and doctrine as this, and contend that the doctrine of the coming or near coming of the Son of man to receive the kingdom, is calculated to produce no such effect upon the mind of his people, but the reverse! for it is the doctrine calculated to fill them with gladness—to make them lift up their heads with joy; for in it they see their redemption drawing nigh—the time when they shall receive the crown of righteousness from the LORD the righteous Judge—"they love His appearing." And when the supremely desired event takes place, when He appears in glory, in the glory-streaming heavens, they will cry in the gladness of their heart—in the raptures of their soul, "Lo, this is our GOD, we have waited for Him, and He will save us; this is the LORD; we have waited for Him, *we will be glad, and rejoice in His salvation.*"

"The righteous, undismayed, and bold—best proof
This day, of fortitude sincere—sustained

By inward faith, with acclamations loud,
Received the coming of the Son of man;
And, drawn by love, inclined to his approach,
Moving to meet the brightness of His face."

CHAPTER V.

BY WHOM THE KINGDOM IS TO BE GIVEN TO MESSIAH—BY THE LORD GOD.

"The Lord God shall give unto Him the throne of His father David; and He shall reign over the house of Jacob for ever; and of His kingdom there shall be no end."—LUKE i. 32, 33.

THE glorious and eternal kingdom to be given to Messiah upon His return to earth, is not in the possession of men, nor to be bestowed by the people. The nation of Israel still in covenant favour with God—the combined kingdoms of the earth, will not, cannot even if they were disposed, which they will not be, bestow the kingdom upon Jesus. According to the angel Gabriel it is to be given to Him by a greater than they ; by the Lord God who created all things, and in whose hand is the breath and destiny of all flesh living. He gave it to Him by covenant and promise, through Abraham, Isaac, Jacob, David, and His virgin mother—He gave it by covenant and promise unto Himself; and at the appointed time, He will give it to Him by actual gift and possession. The Lord has now set Him at His right hand, till He make His enemies His footstool; and after that great work is achieved He will give Him the kingdom. "Ask of me and I will give thee the heathen for thine inheritance, and the uttermost parts of the earth for thy possession. Thou shalt break them with a rod of iron: thou shalt dash them in pieces like a potter's vessel." "He shall judge among the heathen; he shall fill the places with dead bodies; He shall wound the heads over many countries."

These, and many other passages of scripture teach, that the kingdom is to be given to Prince Messiah, by God the Father; but it is deemed unnecessary to enter further into this.

Daniel in vision beheld this glorious transaction;—the Lord God giving the kingdom to the SON of the highest, to Prince Messiah, and describes it in these words, Dan. vii. 13, 14. "I saw in the night visions, and behold one like the Son of Man, came with the clouds of heaven, and came to the Ancient of days, and they brought Him near before Him. And there was given Him dominion, and glory, and a kingdom, that all people, nations and languages should serve Him." According to this then, the kingdom will be given to Messiah, the Son of the highest, the prince of peace by God the Father. And without going further into this, that GOD the father will give the kingdom to Messiah,

His beloved Son, according to the covenant made with Him, He having perfectly fulfilled the conditions of that covenant; it may be remarked that the Lord will give it, as we have seen, at the time when the thrones are set for judgment; when the last remnants of the fourth Monarchy—the ten kingdoms are destroyed. The kingdom which he has purchased, by humiliation, suffering and death: the earth which has been watered by His compassionate sorrowful tears, and baptized with His piacular blood, and redeemed by the merits of the same, shall be given to Him by the father. "I have made a covenant with my chosen, I have sworn unto David my servant, thy SEED will I establish for ever, and build up thy throne to all generations." "The LORD hath sworn in truth unto David, he will not turn from it. Of the FRUIT of thy body will I set upon thy throne." And when the Lord God gives to Messiah, this kingdom His by promise and covenant, His by redemption, He may address Him in sentiments like these, so beautifully expressed by the poet—

"Come then, and added to thy many crowns,
Receive yet one, the crown of all the earth,
Thou who alone art worthy! It was thine
By ancient covenant, ere nature's birth;
And thou hast made it thine by purchase since,
And overpaid its value with thy blood.
Thy saints proclaim THEE KING; and in their hearts
Thy title is engraven with a pen
Dipt in the fountain of eternal love."

In conclusion, it may be remarked, that from all this, there are some very important lessons to be learned, and some very precious consolation to be derived ; and to these it may be proper and profitable briefly to advert.

1. Notice then for a moment the blessedness that shall prevail upon the earth when the kingdom shall be given to the Son of the Highest.

The KING of righteousness, mercy and peace seated upon the throne of His father David, and swaying the sceptre of equity over an emancipated and redeemed world, every petty tyrant that would lord it over his fellow men, shall be crushed to the dust : every arm of oppression that would make the helpless tremble and groan under its power shall be broken, and all enjoy the glorious "liberty of the sons of God"—all feel that they are the freemen of Him, who has redeemed them with His blood, and unite in singing the song, "unto Him that loved us, and washed us from our sins in His own blood ; and hath made us kings and priests unto God, and His father, to Him be glory and dominion for ever and ever." The light of divine truth, streaming in cloudless splendour from the pure fountain of eternal truth—emanating from the face of JESUS like brightness from the sun—chasing away ignorance and error from all hearts and conduct ; the kingdom of the LORD shall shine in unclouded perfection upon every soul, filling all with the enrapturing knowledge of Him. Then shall men know even as they are known.

Hatred too, the offspring of hell, shall find no lurking-place in any bosom ; no home in any heart of any inhabitant of that kingdom, for it is the kingdom of Messiah—the kingdom of pure, holy, sincere universal love. Oh! love is the atmosphere, the law, the language, the very nature of that kingdom, for Christ who is love will be all in all. This omnipresence of divine love, everywhere dominant, and everywhere supremely felt will unite all—all earth's inhabitants in its perfect bliss-inspiring confederacy, and make all perfectly happy in its undisturbed and endless reign, and realize the scene of beauty and bliss so graphically depicted by the Hebrew prophet, and so sweetly poured forth by Israel's harp. "Righteousness shall be the girdle of His loins, and faithfulness the girdle of His reins. The wolf shall dwell with the lamb, and the leopard shall lie down with the kid; and the calf, and the young lion and the fatling together ; and a little child shall lead them. And the cow and the bear shall feed, their young ones shall lie down together; and the lion shall eat straw like the ox. And the sucking child shall play on the hole of the asp, and the weaned child shall put his hand on the cockatrice's den. They shall not hurt nor destroy in all God's holy mountain." Perfect happiness shall have its undisturbed habitation in every breast—shall be the portion of every soul; and every tongue shall join with rapture in the world's epithalamium, when the universal song of love and blessedness ascends to Him, who reigns in righteousness over its redeemed domains, and the cry bursts from the all happy inhabitants, "Behold the tabernacle of God is with men."

2. Notice the duty of waiting for Messiah's coming kingdom.

That it is our duty to wait for the LORD'S coming and kingdom, is made certain by His own teaching, as well as that of His disciples and apostles. Again and again He referred to this event; and referred to it as an event of the very utmost importance to every man—an event of such vast importance, that it ought to be first in our heart and affections; and that preparation for it ought to form the principal, the sole business of life. This duty of such importance and magnitude, Christ frequently inculcated upon His disciples, and the multitude who waited upon His preaching. Ever and anon, we find Him addressing them in words like these, "Be ye also ready, for at such an hour as ye think not the SON of Man cometh." "Watch and pray, for ye know not at what hour the SON of Man will come." Now these and many similar passages, have no reference whatever to death, though they are frequently quoted by many as referring to that event. Such an use or application of these passages is beyond all controversy a gross and unpardonable misapplication of holy scripture. They refer not to death, but to the personal, visible coming of the SON of Man at His return to earth, to receive the kingdom, and sit upon the throne of His father David. And that this is the event to which they refer is palpably manifest from the connexion in which they stand, for CHRIST was not speaking to them of death, but of His coming to judgment at the last day: and also, from the meaning of the Greek word, which literally signifies to be present: to be personally present face to face. This, then, being the true meaning of these passages, CHRIST frequently by command, solemnly imposes upon us, the solemn and important duty of waiting and preparing for His return to earth—to judgment and His kingdom.

The faithful in every age have understood these, and kindred passages as teaching this doctrine, and inculcating this duty; and consequently they waited for and desired the personal coming of the LORD JESUS CHRIST. When the thief in death-agony on the cross was converted, it appears that the glorious coming, and consequent blessedness of Messiah's kingdom was revealed with peculiar clearness to his view, and hence his prayer, "Lord, remember me *when thou comest in thy kingdom.*" His eye looked into the far future, and saw JESUS who then hung by his side upon the cross, coming in the clouds of heaven with power and great glory, the anointed judge of all mankind, and the king of the new creation, and felt the conviction pressing with overwhelming power upon his mind and soul, if CHRIST would only remember him in that day, and take him into His kingdom with Him, he would be supremely and eternally happy; and accordingly he prayed only for this one thing. His petition was answered by the best assurance, that his request would be granted. He replied, "to-day shalt thou be with me in Paradise," which was the guarantee, that when He with all His saints would come into His kingdom, He would be with them. The Thessalonians, after their conversion, turned to God from idols, to serve the living and true God, *and to wait for His Son from heaven,* "whom He raised from the dead." Bishops Bradford, Ridley, Latimer, and other martyrs were comforted and sustained by the same precious truth—they looked for the coming of the Lord. Oh! let us not, then, cherish the infidel feeling, or give utterance to the infidel sentiment, "The LORD delayeth His coming." Let us not regard that event as far distant; but as near at hand. If the Thessalonians, under the immediate teaching and influence of the Holy Spirit, waited for the Son of man from heaven, how much more imperative is this duty upon us who live in these last times:—these times full of the thickening signs of His coming, each having in it a distinct voice intimating the nearness of the event; and all these signs and busy onward movements proclaiming by the mighty noise of their commotions, the preparations in progress for His advent, amidst the din of which, the attentive, listening ear may hear the prelusive sounds of His appearing. Let us not look at death as an event that may intervene; for with that we have nothing to do. The Lord and His disciples never teach or inculcate the duty of watching and waiting and preparing for death, but uniformly for His coming in glory and judgment. It is therefore our supreme duty to be watching and waiting for the personal coming of the Son of Man, and that the more, inasmuch as we see the day drawing nigh; so that we may be ready for it, and even now in our earnest desire to see it, cry with the believing multitude, "COME, LORD JESUS, COME QUICKLY."

Reader, are you watching and waiting for the Lord's personal coming and kingdom? Are you ready for that glorious day and its solemn and unalterable decisions? Oh, seek to be ready! Let nothing prevent you from making the necessary preparation. Give your heart, your time, your all to the work—watch, pray, wait, for at such a time as ye think not the Son of Man cometh.

3. Notice the influence which the certainty of the Father giving the Kingdom to the Son, or the introduction of Christ's kingdom into the earth, should have upon our mind and conduct.

The giving of the kingdom to Christ, or its introduction into the earth; or the personal coming of the Son of man, which are one and the same thing, is the grand divine argument everywhere advanced throughout the New Testament to persuade and urge men to the performance of every duty; and to encourage and sustain and comfort Christians under all their trials. The argument to persuade to the performance of duty, and the consolation to sustain under severe trials, is not the shortness of life and the certainty and nearness of death. These may be advanced by men, and are frequently advanced by men ; but they are not divine but human arguments, and consequently powerless, worthless.

God's arguments to persuade and urge men to the performance of duty—to attend promptly, faithfully to the great business of life ; and his consolations to sustain them under the sufferings and trials of such a life are all drawn from the glorious coming of the Son of man to judgment, or something connected with that coming. A few examples may suffice to illustrate the truth of these remarks. Is repentance a work necessary to the reception of the Saviour and obtaining eternal life ; the great duty inculcated upon impenitent, perishing men ? The coming of the Son of man to judgment is the mighty argument to persuade to the performance of this duty ; John cried to the multitude waiting upon his ministry, "Repent ye, for the *kingdom of heaven is at hand ;*" Matt. iii. 2. Peter when enforcing the same duty upon the Jews for crucifying the Lord of glory said, "Repent ye therefore, and be converted, that your sins may be blotted out, when the time of refreshing shall come from the presence of the Lord, and *He shall send Jesus Christ,* who before was preached unto you, whom the heavens must receive until the times of the restitution of all things ;" Acts iii. 19–21. Is love to Christ, which gives heart and affection all to Him, the great and glorious duty inculcated ? His coming is the argument to obedience. "If any man love not the

Lord Jesus Christ, let him be Anathema Maranatha;" which being interpreted is, "Let him be accursed—*our Lord cometh;*" 1 Cor xvi. 22. Are men exhorted to mortify their lusts and live lives of faith and holiness? It is by the coming of the Lord. "The grace of God that bringeth salvation hath appeared to all men, teaching us, that denying ungodliness and worldly lusts we should live soberly, righteously, and godly in this present evil world; looking for that blessed hope, (*even*) *the glorious appearing* of the great GOD and our SAVIOUR JESUS CHRIST;" Tit. ii. 11–13. Is holiness inculcated —purity in heart and life—conformity to the character of the Saviour? It is by the coming of the Lord. "We know that *when He shall appear* we shall be like Him, for we shall see Him as He is. And every man that hath this hope in him purifieth himself even as He is pure;" 1 John iii. 2, 3. Are works of mercy, acts of kindness, benevolence to the poor inculcated? It is by the coming of the Lord, as is clearly taught in the last parable of the twenty-fifth chapter of Matthew's gospel. Is watchfulness inculcated? It is by the coming of the LORD. "Watch, therefore, for ye know neither the day nor the hour *when the* SON *of man cometh;*" Matt. xxv. 13. Are patience and long-suffering amidst all the troubles and trials of the present life, and self-denial and persecutions of the Christian warfare inculcated? It is by the coming of the Lord and the recompense that shall be awarded on that day. "Be patient, therefore, brethren, unto the *coming* of the LORD. Behold the husbandman waiteth for the precious fruit of the earth, and hath long patience for it, until he receive the early and latter rain. Be ye also patient, stablish your heart, for the *coming of the Lord draweth nigh;*" Jas. v. 7, 8. Are ministerial fidelity and diligence, unwearied labours to win souls to CHRIST inculcated? It is by the coming of the LORD. "I charge thee therefore, before God and the LORD JESUS CHRIST, who shall judge the quick and the dead *at His appearing* and His kingdom; preach the word, be instant in season and out of season; reprove, rebuke, exhort with all long-suffering and doctrine;" 2 Tim. iv. 1, 2. Is consolation offered to those who are mourning the loss of Christian friends, and weeping because the grave has hidden those whom they loved from their eyes? This consolation, too, is offered through the *coming* of the LORD. "But I would not have you to be ignorant, brethren, concerning them which are asleep, that ye sorrow not even as others which have no hope. For if we believe that Jesus died and rose again, even so them also, which sleep in JESUS, will God *bring with Him.* For this we say unto you by the word of the Lord, that we which are alive and remain unto the *coming of the* LORD shall not prevent them which are asleep;" 1 Thess. iv. 13–15. Is consolation amidst trials, persecutions, or in the prospect of death administered? It is by rewards to be bestowed at the *coming* of the Son of man. "Henceforth, there is laid up for me a crown of righteousness which the LORD, the righteous Judge, shall give me at that day ; and not to me only, but unto all them also that love his appearing ;" 2 Tim. iv. 8. "When the chief SHEPHERD shall appear, ye shall receive a crown of glory that fadeth not away ;" 1 Pet. v. 4.

From this very hasty view and meagre outline of examples, it does appear manifest that the second and glorious coming of the Son of man is the grand argument of Scripture and of infinite Wisdom, who knows best what will operate most readily, most certainly, most powerfully upon the mind and consciences of men, to persuade to the full and faithful performance of every duty ; and the source of supreme consolation to every believer amidst all the trials of the Christian life. And if this be the case, as it certainly is, then it is the obvious duty of every one to keep the grand and glorious event of CHRIST coming to judgment, coming to His kingdom, before his mind, that by its mighty stirring influence, he may be urged on amidst all the discouragements in his way, to the faithful and persevering performance of every duty, and be sustained amid all trials by its abounding consolation.

Reader, turn your eye to that most glorious event, which will soon fill heaven and earth with its dazzling and awful glory, the personal coming of the LORD of glory to judgment and His kingdom. Contemplate that scene of unutterable, inconceivable, divine splendour and majesty, affecting, changing all things on earth. Endeavour to realize it, for it shall soon in all its ineffable grandeur be unfolded to your view. Soon the eye that traces these lines, the immortal being that ponders these truths, shall behold the Son of man bursting from these heavens which have so long received Him, His eyes like a flame of fire, and on His head many crowns; accompanied, surrounded by the radiant, happy multitude which no man can number, saved out of all nations, kindreds, and tongues, "clothed in linen clean and white;" and the myriads of His holy angels, whose vast numbers and outspread wings cover the whole heavens, and the glory of the glorious LORD pouring in floods of brightness all around. Soon you shall hear the awful, the dead-awakening, the grave-opening voice of the Archangel and the trump of GOD, pealing their omnipotent notes from the excessive brightness of the terrible glory of the descending Judge, "whose throne is like the fiery flame and His wheels like burning fire;" and see as these roll round the earth, the tombs opening, the dead awakening, and hurrying in vast numbers from their dark beds; the earth, the great metropolis of the dead everywhere heaving with the mighty impulses of life, and pouring forth her countless, deathless swarms. As he approaches you shall see earth's stable and mighty military guarded thrones shake and tumble to the dust—crowns which have long decked the head of Majesty and been the ornament, the pride, if not the god of the haughty wearer, fall from the brow of earthly sovereignty and be trodden under foot, worthless and despised things—sceptres for the obtaining of which seas of human blood have been shed, and many plains strewed with the dead—which have been seized with eager hand and held with life grasp, tossed away, useless by those who so vehemently desired them. You shall see Antichrist, who has been drunken with the blood of the saints, given to the unquenchable flame, and consumed with devouring burning—the mother of abominations cast into the lake of fire and brimstone—the smoke of her torment ascending—hear the saints exclaiming in rapture over her doom and the infliction of her righteous punishment; "Allelujah! allelujah, for the LORD GOD omnipotent reigneth."

Ah! yes, reader, you shall soon see all this, nor shall you be an isolated, a disinterested spectator. You shall have your place in all this; but where will your place be? what will your situation be? You will not, cannot be an uninterested spectator. Ah! no. You will hold a place in the scenes of that day, and the place which you occupy will involve your destiny for eternity. At that time the throne of David shall be built up, and the SON of the Highest shall ascend that throne; and He with His redeemed and glorified saints take possession of the renewed earth, and the reign of CHRIST and His saints, a reign of more than Paradisiacal glory and blessedness begin,—a reign which shall have no end. Oh, reader, will you be among the glorified saints that will inherit that kingdom? Have you believed in CHRIST? Is your soul washed in His blood and clothed in his righteousness? Have you all your arrangements and preparations completed for the coming of the Son of man and the decisions of that day? Oh! be persuaded amidst all the bustle and turmoil of the present vanishing life, to keep your eye ever turned to that event—ever steadfastly fixed upon it—endeavour habitually to realize it, live, act, as if the scene were visible over your head, and you were winding up the great business of life in the increasing flood of its resplendent glory—ready to welcome your coming Lord and with Him enter in triumph and glory into His kingdom.

THE END.

www.ingramcontent.com/pod-product-compliance
Lightning Source LLC
LaVergne TN
LVHW050528100826
845148LV00002B/478